T0284545

Christ
ON THE
Psych
Ward

DAVID FINNEGAN-HOSEY

Church Publishing
NEW YORK

Unless otherwise noted, the Scripture quotations contained herein are from the New Revised Standard Version Bible, copyright © 1989 by the Division of Christian Education of the National Council of Churches of Christ in the U.S.A. Used by permission. All rights reserved.

Church Publishing
19 East 34th Street
New York, NY 10016
www.churchpublishing.org

Cover design by Paul Soupiset
Typeset by Rose Design

Library of Congress Cataloging-in-Publication Data

A record of this book is available from the Library of Congress.

ISBN-13: 978-0-89869-051-4 (pbk.)
ISBN-13: 978-0-89869-052-1 (ebook)

Printed in the United States of America

Contents

This book is dedicated to:
My parents, who helped me tell stories;
Leigh, who helped me tell this one;
and Miss Chalfant, because I promised.

Ad Majorem Dei Gloriam

Gratitude

Any book takes a village to bring it to publication. In the case of this book, I'm conscious that it first took a village to keep me alive and healthy in order to be able to write it. My deep gratitude extends to all those who were present with me during the events described in this book. To all the friends, family, classmates, housemates, clergy, congregation members, doctors, nurses, social workers, and counselors who were there for me: thank you. To everyone who drove me to the hospital, visited me, helped me move, wrote to me, spent time with me, and prayed for me: thank you. The very fact that there are too many of you to name is grace of the most amazing kind.

This book would not exist without the work of Milton Brasher-Cunningham, my editor at Church Publishing. Milton not only edited the project but also advocated for it and encouraged me in my writing. Mike Stavlund connected me to Milton and offered advice and encouragement. Teresa Pasquale Mateus encouraged me to apply to speak at Wild Goose and Sarah Griffith Lund invited me to share the stage with her. Sarah and Teresa, along with Robert Saler, Marion Hosey, and Deb Hosey White, reviewed early versions of the book proposal and provided counsel, encouragement, and support. Carole Sargent of Georgetown University provided important guidance early in my writing process.

Several sections of this book first came to life as class projects at Wesley Theological Seminary. My thanks in particular to Dr. Denise Dombkowski Hopkins, Dr. Sharon Ringe, Dr. Michael Koppel, and Dr. Josiah Young for creating the classroom contexts in which these ideas could find their way into words. Special thanks to Dr. Cedric Johnson for giving me the opportunity to present some these ideas to his class during my time as his teaching assistant. Dr. Christine Wade, my undergraduate thesis advisor at Washington College in Chestertown, Maryland, introduced me to liberation theology and gave me the best writing advice I've ever received. The students I have worked with at American University, Wesley Theological Seminary, and Georgetown University have taught and inspired me during the writing of this book. I am grateful for their curiosity, their questions, and their courage. I am also grateful for Rev. Mark Schaefer of American University, whose phrase "solidarity is salvation" is featured in the poem that gives this book its name.

Many thanks to my Patreon supporters, who allowed me to dedicate time and energy to writing: Marion and Gary Hosey, Judy and Eric Sarriot, Stephanie Rogers, Krista Parker, Jane Finnegan, Monica Nehls, Louise Carr, Carissa Surber, Johanna Sarriot, Anne Hosey and Scott Carlton, Sylvia Schneider and Jeff Briggs, Samantha Larson, Laura Martin, and Jen Southworth. In addition, my thanks to everyone who read my blog and wrote me to let me know my words had meaning for them.

Books have soundtracks. This book's soundtrack was provided by the bands Poor Clare and mewithoutYou, to whom I am profoundly grateful.

No compilation of gratitude would be complete without expressing a thousand thanks to Leigh Finnegan-Hosey, for her mental, emotional, spiritual, and material support throughout this entire process. Without Leigh, this book would never have been written. Thank you to our dog, Penny Lane, who kept me company during long hours of writing. Finally, completely, thank you to the One who breathes life into our lungs and grace into our lives. Your grace truly is sufficient for me.

Let Me Tell You a Story

My parents helped me tell stories.

Whatever else there is to say, it starts here—with my mom and my dad, listening to me spin fanciful tales about Martians and dragons and superheroes. Helping me write them down. Helping me illustrate them with crayons and magic markers. Helping me staple the pages from our old dot matrix printer, with the perforated strips on either side that had to be patiently torn away, in between two pieces of light blue construction paper. They would ask me the title and write it in black marker on the front, to make a book of stories. My stories.

Twenty years later, I slumped in a stuffed chair outside of my room in Sibley Hospital's Ward 7 West—the psych ward. My eyes, unfocused and disinterested, traced the patterns in the muted green carpeting. The colors: pastel, inoffensive. My mom sat; my dad stood.

"What do you remember about me as a kid?" I asked. We were trying to piece together the shattered things, to make some sort of sense, some sort of pattern, out of the mess I was in.

"I remember that you were a really happy kid," my mom said. She drew a smiley face—a cartoon depiction of me as a child, a caricature we used to draw to represent me, with over-sized ears and cowlicks, the beginning of a timeline we were crafting on a yellow legal pad.

A really happy kid. Soccer and Sunday school. Games of make-believe and church plays. That's where I begin. A really happy kid, whose parents helped him write and draw his stories.

During my second hospitalization in the summer of 2011, as the hospital was buffeted with the dissipating winds of Hurricane Irene, I wrote these words in one of the dozens of journals I filled with manic scribbling:

> When I was younger, I took a class on creative writing.
>
> At that point in my life, I knew—just *knew*—that I was going to be a novelist when I grew up, and that I would write science fiction and fantasy stories that would be wildly popular.
>
> "Write what you know," the instructor said. And I was in awe of the people in my class who knew something worthwhile to write about. One girl described the light sides of the leaves blowing up, up—a sign of an impending hurricane. Not anything I knew anything about. And as I watch the leaves do just that, today, as the outskirts of Hurricane Irene blow past the psych ward windows, I realize how much I have changed.
>
> I used to have no patience for stories about anything other than the wild imaginings of my childhood—Martians and centaurs, gods and moons. Now, I can't imagine writing about anything outside the walls of this place—its subdued, dark colors, green and mauve, 1970s-keep-them-calm colors. Rounded everything—rounded shower rails, rounded toilet paper holders, and on and on . . . nothing to hang yourself from.
>
> And I am writing by the bright sunlight of the window overlooking the glistening water. And if I can just imagine, for a second, imagine not Martians or elves but just imagine that I'm not overlooking a water treatment plant, then maybe for this moment I can be beautiful and whole and ok.
>
> Light on water—O how I have wrecked things, some days.
>
> "Write what you know," my teacher said. And increasingly I wonder if what that really means for me is: "Write nothing. Watch the light on the water. Listen to the sound of the wind."

As it turns out, I am congenitally incapable of writing nothing, of not telling a story. And so, I will write what I know: The story of a happy kid, a church kid, who found himself in seminary and then found himself in the psych ward, and now finds himself wondering what the latter place has to teach the former places.

This is my story, or a piece of it at least. The story I know. When I write about my experiences with mental health, mental illness, and faith, this is where I'm coming from. My story is not one of massive trauma, nor systemic oppression. Those stories must be told, and heard, but I am not the one to tell them. There are other voices, other storytellers, to speak from those places of hurt, from those hot forges of identity. All our stories, in all their multiplicity and layers, must be told, not simply for their own sakes, but because telling our stories of mental health and mental illness, of hurt and resilience, of despair and healing, is a powerful act of resistance in a culture of silence and isolation. Mental illness is an experience of fragmentation and alienation. It shatters our narratives and forces us into the hardest task of our lives: to somehow reintegrate all these broken bits into some kind of whole. To try to make some sense of it, out loud or on paper or on canvas, to try somehow to forge communication and connection out of silence and stigma, is the sort of counterhegemonic, counterintuitive act that the word "gospel" is meant to describe. To find words, to choose the pen instead of the razor, is a victory. An act of resistance. Good news to be shouted from the mountaintop. An announcement to be carried by the swift feet of messengers. To tell our stories. To tell my story.

This book is an attempt to model vulnerability.

More than ten years ago, during my sophomore year of college, I asked one of my pastors and mentors, Rev. Karen Thomas Smith, to describe her job to me. My only rule was she couldn't use any "churchy language." I knew she led worship, presided at communion, taught Bible studies, but I wanted to know what she really *did*.

Karen pondered for a moment before answering, and then responded, "I try to model vulnerability."

It's been more than a decade since I heard those words, and they've been with me ever since. I'm not sure I knew what they meant at the time. Perhaps I still don't. Still, something about Karen's answer resonated with me, struck a deep chord in my soul. Modeling vulnerability meant I didn't have to have all the answers, answers I had often demanded from the church. It meant not having it all together, which I certainly did not, and no amount of participation in Christian community has changed that. It meant I didn't have to be right all the time, which was a shift for me since being right, I confess, has often been one of my core motivations.

In a way, since that conversation with Karen, I've been trying to respond to the call to model vulnerability. A vulnerable call, from a vulnerable God, to a vulnerable ministry, in a vulnerable church—willing to take risks, to expose one's self, to share out instead of closing in.

This book emerges from my journey with mental health struggles, but, ultimately, vulnerability is what this book is about. Sharing my story is an exercise in vulnerability. Just as important, the images, reflections, and fragments of thoughts about God and faith and ministry that have stumbled their way out of the labyrinth of my personal story are tied together, not by a particular diagnosis, but by the theme of vulnerability. What my story reveals, if it reveals anything at all, are hints of a more vulnerable understanding of God and faith than much of what has been common in the mainstream Christian discourse of our present age. When I look at the Christian story, I see at its center a vulnerable God, a God in tension with the ways we have classically described the divine, a God far too susceptible to suffering and surprise to fit too comfortably into the clothing of omniscience, omnipotence, or omnibenevolence. The God whom I have met along my journey with mental illness, disguised often in a stranger's face, a community's embrace, or the long and lonely darkness of a sleepless night, is a God whose vulnerability creates the conditions for solidarity with those struggling, hurting, and wondering why.

Recent work by the popular speaker and social researcher Brené Brown has revealed the importance of vulnerability for parenting, leadership, and a host of other disciplines.[1] Vulnerability, Brown argues, while at the core of human experiences of shame and fear, is also at the core of courageous, compassionate, and authentic living.[2] Church practitioners such as the Rev. Amy Butler of Riverside Church in New York City have already begun working out some of the implications for this vulnerability research in the field of practical ministry.[3] In telling my own story, I hope to provide a glimpse of what vulnerability might mean in terms of a faith that can survive—albeit a bit battered, a bit fragmented—the afflictions of mental illness. Such a faith, I suspect, is also what is needed for a church that can survive—albeit a bit battered, a bit fragmented—the changes and challenges of the next few decades.

In the pages that follow, I will tell some part of my personal story of mental health and illness, faith and doubt, healing and struggle. This story is mine. I cannot speak for all people with mental illness. The suffering I have experienced in terms of mental health is real; at the same time, I speak from a certain place of privilege. The particular form of mental illness that I've been diagnosed with has proven relatively responsive to treatment, which is not the case for all who suffer. What's more, I have had access, in terms of both finances and information, to treatment, which is also not the case for all who suffer. I have been surrounded by supportive friends, family, and faith communities, which is quite remarkable given the isolating effect that mental illness tends to have. The other forms of societal privilege that I carry—my (white) race, my (cis male) gender identity, my (hetero)sexuality—mean I have not had to grapple with the multiplying effects of other forms of oppression that many who experience mental and emotional crisis have to face. This is my story, and mine alone.

At the same time, as I wrestle with my own experiences of mental health struggles and the way I believe those experiences have revealed divine activity, I cannot help but connect my story to broader themes and broader conversations. I will sometimes refer to people with mental illness, or people with mental health struggles, knowing even as I do that what I say may not always resonate, may miss the point, may fall short. There is nothing final or total or infallible about the reflections I offer here. I pray that by sharing these thoughts, I open up some space for others to share their own stories.

Why tell this story now? And whom am I telling it for?

Those questions, unsurprisingly, require their own story. In the summer of 2015, I was invited to present at the Wild Goose Festival in Hot Springs, North Carolina, a Christian gathering that describes itself as a "Spirit, Justice, Music and Arts Festival." My co-presenter Rev. Sarah Lund and I planned a talk about mental health, mental illness, and spirituality. Wild Goose, as the name might indicate, is an exercise in organized, creative, chaos. There are always multiple speakers, musicians, artists, and storytellers in multiple tents at any given time. Our talk was scheduled at the same time as a presentation on the main stage of the festival that featured several very well-known national figures. I figured that if ten people showed up, it would be ok; if twenty people showed up, it would a big success; if fifty people showed up, we could take a victory lap. Something more like three hundred and fifty people showed up. We packed the tent to overflowing. One of the organizers told us later that we had one of the largest crowds in the space of the whole weekend. I was stunned.

What was remarkable about the talk was how very unremarkable either Sarah's or my story were. Sarah had just published a book on her family's journey with mental illness,[4] but was certainly not a headlining name at the festival; I was unpublished, new to the festival, a complete unknown. The hundreds of people who crowded into the tent to hear us did not come because of name recognition. They came because they wanted, needed, desperately longed for, a space to share stories they were used to clutching tightly inside of their broken hearts. Especially in church. Especially in Christian spaces.

At the end of our presentation, we invited people to turn to each other in groups of two or three to share their own stories. People stayed long after our talk was supposed to be over. Their need was palpable. They were family members of people struggling. They were people with suffering of their own, often hidden. They were people in search, not so much of answers, but of places where even asking the questions or tentatively sharing the story would be okay, even welcomed. After the talk was over, several people said they hoped I would write a book about the experiences I had shared. It was not so much their direct statements but the feeling in that tent—the need, the longing, the pain and hope present in that space—that finally got me to sit down and start typing. To try, as my parents had helped me to do decades ago, to make a book of my stories.

I am telling this story, first and foremost for—or maybe with—fellow strugglers with mental health problems. I cannot claim to speak on behalf of all people with mental health problems, and will strive not to. Yet, if telling our stories is an act of resistance to the alienation and isolation of mental illness, then to share my story is to participate in that resistance. I hope to be one more voice breaking the silence, one more crack in the dividing wall of stigma, so that one day people with mental illness and mental health struggles will not have to experience either the silence or the stigma.

This story is also for the family and friends of those of us who struggle. As with many people who struggle with mental health problems, there is no neat division in my life between sufferer, family member, and friend. I am all of the above. I have seen the suffering caused by mental illness in members of my family and have often had no idea how to respond. I have had friends paralyzed by depression and anxiety and I have said things that have been unhelpful, even hurtful. My story is for all of us—co-strugglers, co-sojourners, on a difficult journey.

I am also writing for churches and ministers who are wondering how to be in ministry with people struggling with mental health problems. I write both as a person of faith and as someone whose vocational life has been oriented toward church and ministry. My orientation informs my writing, and I will offer resources, or at least guideposts, for those who share it.

This is also a book for the church as a whole, or at least for the church in the context most familiar to me, the church in the United States. Anyone paying attention knows that churches in the U.S. are currently faced with a plethora of challenges. The surprising good news I offer is that those struggling with mental health problems have important lessons and insights to offer the church, and they are exactly the sort of lessons and insights that might help churches be faithful in the challenging environment in which they find themselves.

In her book *Queer Virtue,* Episcopal priest Elizabeth M. Edman makes two claims that powerfully and provocatively set the stage for her overall argument:

> I started this book because I observed two things: first, my queer identity has taught me more about how to be a good *Christian* than has the church. . . . The second observation that got me writing is a question: If my queer identity informs my understanding of my Christian faith, might the lessons of queer identity help other Christians better understand their faith, too? I feel this question rear its head whenever I am part of the discussions about addressing the spiritual needs of a particular group of people: gay people, survivors

of intimate partner violence, people affected by HIV/AIDS, and others. In these discussions, I often perceive a dynamic, an attitude, that I find uncomfortable: that there is some spiritual authority outside the experience of these people, and that this authority, if tapped, will benefit the people as they live into the particularity of their collaborative experience. Conversations about spiritual experience should with far greater regularity move in the opposite direction.[5]

I by no means wish to conflate the LGBTQ community with those who struggle with mental health problems. They are distinct experiences, although those with mental illness exist in every other type of community, and the particular struggles and trauma faced by certain communities must be heard and understood in any work toward holistic mental health. As Edman suggests, however, I wish for the conversation about mental illness and the church to "move in the opposite direction." Rather than a conversation about people with mental illness, and how the church can help them, I want the church to listen to and hear the stories of people with mental illness, and to discover the surprising gifts we have to offer. As Edman writes, "I want to encourage people who claim the mantle of Christianity to hone our ability to receive and embrace such perspectives as essential to the vivification of our tradition."[6] I hope this book can contribute to such a vivifying conversation.

Throughout the chapters that follow, I will use various terms to refer to my experience. You will hear me use the terms "mental health struggles," "mental health challenges," "mental health problems," as well as the term "mental illness." While related and overlapping, these terms are not entirely interchangeable. I use "mental illness," as well as "mood disorders," to refer to the sort of clinical diagnosis found in the *Diagnostic and Statistical Manual of Mental Disorders*, or DSM, the text which psychiatrists and other medical doctors use to diagnose and treat patients. A remarkable number of people in the

U.S. will receive an official diagnosis some time in their lives. "Mental health struggles," "challenges," or "problems" however, are universal. Everyone has physical health, and everyone has a challenge or struggle related to their health at some time during their lives. Everyone has mental health, as well as the accompanying challenges of maintaining mental health. The relationship between mental health and mental illness will be discussed in greater detail in Chapter 8.

While I recognize it is linguistically cumbersome, at times, to use the phrase "people with mental illness" or "people with mental health struggles," I choose to use this phrasing rather than referring to "the mentally ill." Those of us with mental illnesses are people first. We are not our illness. That said, individuals make different choices in how to refer to themselves, and I believe these choices are empowering and need to be heard and respected.[7] In a similar vein, in discussions of suicide, I avoid referring to people as "suicides" and try not to use the terms "committed suicide" or "attempted suicide." One "commits" a murder—a crime; one "attempts" something and can either succeed or fail, which seems the wrong framework in discussing the painful reality of suicide. Just as some might succumb to a potentially lethal illness while others might survive, I will refer to people who have "died by suicide" or who have "survived suicide."[8]

I will refer to my own diagnosis quite often: Type II Bipolar Disorder, or bipolar II for short. For me, this diagnosis has been helpful in many ways. However, I agree whole-heartedly with pastor and theologian Monica A. Coleman, herself someone with bipolar II, who writes:

> My diagnosis is just shorthand and not my fully developed story. It's only a very brief way of explaining some of what I live with. It's probably most helpful for psychiatrists. Mental health conditions are as unique as the people who live with them. . . . More importantly, my diagnosis is just one part

of what can be said about me. There's a lot more to me than this name. This name was given to me by people who write manuals.[9]

Chapter 7 will delve into this topic in greater depth.

If you think language about mental health and mental illness is confusing, brace yourself. It's time to talk about language for God! Since this book emerges out of my own experience as a person of faith, specifically the Christian faith, and since it is written at least in part with churches and those in Christian ministry in mind, I use Christian language throughout. Of course, with two thousand years of Christian tradition (and six thousand years of the Jewish tradition, out of which Christianity emerged), there is no single definition of "Christian language." You will find scripture quotations and references to theologians throughout this book, as well as many discussions of the ways I understand and give name to my experience of the divine.

I generally avoid using masculine or feminine language for God, although Chapter 5 will discuss this topic in much greater detail and will point out the importance of feminine images of God. Sometimes, avoiding masculine language— particularly male pronouns ("he," "him," or "his")—for God can be complicated or sound repetitive; nevertheless, I think it is an important choice. In the introduction to her own spiritual account of bipolar disorder, Episcopal priest Kathryn Greene-McCreight writes that she chooses not to use inclusive language for God because "it is not the nature of the Christian God to 'include' either males or females within its being in this way."[10] Greene-McCreight's book is beautiful and enormously helpful, and I resonate with her statement that the scriptural and theological aspects of her writing are "integral to the book, not just frosting."[11] However, I find myself in disagreement with her not only in the question of language but also, as I hope the reader will discover, in our understandings of the divine. It will be my contention throughout this book that it is exactly the nature of the Christian God to include suffering humanity, in radical, scandalous, and vulnerable ways; and that just such an understanding of God was the one I discovered underneath the rubble that mental illness caused in my life. If Christ is indeed on the psych ward standing in solidarity with suffering humanity and making the divine presence known, then God is not a distant figure separated from humanity by a chasm of difference, but is rather an embracing, inclusive presence. Surely such a presence can transcend the bounds of gender, and certainly of gendered language.

Mental illness is an experience of fragmentation, and so I have tried to avoid crafting too neat a story or tying up too many loose ends. Instead of a continuous narrative, what follows in these pages is the weaving together of three interconnected threads. The first thread, my personal testimony of mental illness and healing, is told both through narration and through a scattering of poetry and journal entries from repeated hospitalizations during the second half of 2011. The second is a series of theological reflections, from a Christian perspective, of how we come to understand the presence, or lack thereof, of God in the midst of suffering. The third thread suggests practical implications for faith communities hoping to be in ministry with people who struggle with mental illness. For me, these three threads intertwine with no clear separations or neat boundaries. Thus, this book is not divided into three sections, nor is it arranged chronologically. Instead, each chapter contains a series of memories and reflections and practical ponderings, arranged around a certain theme. The themes, and thus the chapters, are paired with each other in tension and conversation.

In chapter 1, I'll reflect on God's presence; in chapter 2, God's absence will take a paradoxical sort of center stage. Chapter 3 speaks of the core theological concept of sin and the core experiential concept of "not enough;" Chapter 4, of the core theological concept of grace and the core experiential concept of "enough." Chapter 5 will focus on images of God; chapter 6, on images and understandings of ministry and the practical implications of these images. Chapter 7 will explore the way we understand and imagine illness; Chapter 8 will look at a variety of images of healing and recovery. A concluding chapter will draw connections between the Christ I met on the psych ward and the vocation of the church in today's world.

My hope is that my story will resonate with your story, or the story of someone you love, or someone you are struggling to love. "The story of my journey," writes Quaker educator and author Parker Palmer, "is no more or less important than anyone else's. It is simply the best source of data I have on a subject where generalizations often fail but truth may be found in the details."[12] So I offer the following, in all its details—one part testimony, one part theological reflection, and one part prayer—in hopes that a healing conversation about mental health and mental illness can grow in our church and in our world. This is too important a topic, and too needful a conversation, for folks such as myself—who operate in an odd space of privilege even as we learn to live with a brain that sometimes seems out to kill us—to stay silent anymore.

Let me tell you a story.

Notes

1. Brené Brown, *Daring Greatly: How the Courage to be Vulnerable Transforms the Way We Live, Love, Parent, and Lead* (New York: Gotham, 2012).

2. Ibid., 11.

3. Amy Butler, "TMI: Vulnerable Leadership Can Be a Powerful Tool for Building Christian Community. But Can Pastors Go Too Far?," *Baptist News Global*, February 10, 2015, *https://baptistnews.com/opinion/columns/item/29803-tmi.*

4. Sarah Griffith Lund, *Blessed Are the Crazy: Breaking the Silence about Mental Illness, Family, and Church* (St. Louis: Chalice Press, 2014).

5. Elizabeth M. Edman, *Queer Virtue: What LGBTQ People Know about Life and Love and How It Can Revitalize Christianity* (Boston: Beacon Press, 2016), 4–5.

6. Ibid., 5.

7. For a wonderfully accessible explanation of this topic, see this comic by Christine Deneweth, "I'm Schizophrenic, Not 'A Person with Schizophrenia'—So Please Stop Correcting Me," *Everyday Feminism*, November 15, 2015, *http://everydayfeminism.com /2015/11/telling-people-how-to-identify/*.

8. I am indebted to Rev. Dr. James T. Clemmons for this insight and terminology. See *Children of Jonah: Personal Stories by Survivors of Suicide Attempts* (Sterling, VA: Capital Books, 2001), xx.

9. Monica A. Coleman, *Not Alone: Reflections on Faith and Depression* (Culver City, CA: Inner Prizes, 2012), 13–14.

10. Kathryn Greene-McCreight, *Darkness Is My Only Companion: A Christian Response to Mental Illness* (Grand Rapids, MI: Brazos Press, 2015), xiv.

11. Ibid., xiii.

12. Parker Palmer, *Let Your Life Speak: Listening for the Voice of Vocation* (San Francisco: John Wiley & Sons, 2000), 19.

1

Christ on the Psych Ward

n June of 2011 I had the worst week of my life. By most outside indicators, I shouldn't have been miserable. I had just finished my first year of seminary. I'd done well in my classes,
made new friends, and secured the unheard of Holy Grail of
a paid internship at a nearby congregation. So why did it feel
like my life was falling apart?

Looking back, I can list off the triggers, the seemingly small
chips and cracks in the façade of wellbeing I was living behind.
The impending departure of beloved roommates, a series of
relationship failures, a week of on-hold frustration with our
internet provider—all of these seemed, for me, to be indicators
of something deeper and more dangerous, out of proportion to
their individual surmountability. Rather than a series of isolated
challenges, I interpreted the bumps and bruises of that summer
as evidence of my failure: failure to transition into adulthood,
perhaps; failure to figure out life tasks and relationships; failure,
somehow, to live and love. And so it was that I found myself isolated in my basement apartment in Northeast DC, wrapped in
darkness, planning how to end my life. Looking back at a journal entry from that summer, I can watch myself trying to recon-
struct exactly what happened, to craft some sort of coherent
narrative out of a time that felt completely fragmented and jagged. My memories of that time have a surreal quality to them, as
if I am watching distorted footage of someone else's life. What I
know is, at some point, I began to harm myself, something I had
done in high school but thought I had left in the past.

The week progressed—perhaps I should say regressed. I barely slept. Every morning I dragged myself out of bed, primarily by screaming at myself internally. I would go for a run in the heat and humidity of the DC summer, hoping in some strange sense that this would shock me out of my self-destructive state—or maybe, simply, that it would kill me. I stood on the edges of Metro platforms, daring myself to jump in front of incoming trains. In the afternoons, I went to class, appearing to all but the closest of my friends to be doing quite well, absorbing the difficult material of biblical Hebrew. A few hours of studying afterwards with classmates, and then I would return home where I, once again, was isolated in my dark apartment, turning violently inward, falling into pieces and hoping I could work up the courage to die. I was terrified. I had no idea what was going on.

Sometime toward the end of the week, some instinct for self-preservation or longing for life—in the theological language of my Christian tradition, perhaps an encounter with prevenient grace—combined with some foggy awareness of the similarities between this experience and previous struggles with mental health led me to call a suicide hotline. I have no memory of what the person on the other end of the line said, though I am very grateful for them. They talked to me for an hour, before helping me identify a friend I could call. My friend Lindsey had phoned earlier that day; her missed call was still indicated on my phone. She was on the West Coast, and might still be awake. Lindsey picked up the phone and talked me through the night, until I was exhausted enough to fall into a half-sleep. Before I did, she made me promise to call her in the morning and check-in.

I'm a rules follower. I was that tattling kid that got on everyone's nerves in elementary school. In this case, it was a godsend. Lindsey had established a clear "call me in the morning" rule, and so I had to call her, no matter if I wanted to or not. The morning was no better. I found myself examining a bottle of non-prescription pills to see if the warning label gave any description of how lethal an overdose might be. I called Lindsey. We made a list of people close by that I could call. After making a number of calls that went unanswered, I finally reached an acquaintance that served as a chaplain at a nearby university. He came to pick me up and took me to a hospital in DC, where I admitted myself into a psychiatric unit for the first time in my life. It wouldn't be the last.

"I admitted myself into a psychiatric unit."

It's a short, simple sentence; it was neither a short nor a simple process. The whole experience had a surreal element to it, as if I was watching some sort of satirical take on my life rather than living through the experience myself. After I checked in at the ER desk and waited for a while, I was taken to a hospital room. My chaplain friend, perhaps by the power invested in him by his clergy collar, was able to accompany me. I was assigned a nurse intern, and I figured out rather quickly that her job was to observe me and make sure I didn't harm myself. I asked her if she had to write down what I did, and when she said yes, I started cracking jokes, even dancing at one point, to see what would make it into the log. That I was both feeling suicidal and also cracking jokes and interacting with the medical staff should have been a hint that the initial diagnosis of a Major Depressive Disorder was not an accurate description of my condition. In hindsight, I can see now that I was manic, but at the time I had no idea what that meant. If I had any idea what a "manic episode" was, I probably thought it involved delusions or other experiences that I wasn't having. Now I know there is a distinction in the psychiatric world between "hypermania" and "hypomania," but those words meant nothing to me as I sat in the ER.

I was in that room in the ER for hours, with that poor beleaguered nurse intern having to put up with me. A nurse came, then a doctor, to look at the cuts and scratches and burns on my arms and shoulders and stomach. Then a social worker came to ask me a dozen questions, which came down to, "Do you want to kill yourself?" and "Are you willing to voluntarily check yourself into the psychiatric ward?"

"Yeah," I remember thinking, "that's what I came here to do."

I eventually learned that the reason I was waiting was that there wasn't an empty bed in Ward 7 West, but that there was a chance one would open up. And so we waited. Finally, the good news came through—good news that people in my situation don't always get to hear: a bed had opened up. I could go to the psych ward. It was a strange sort of gospel to receive. My chaplain friend and I were escorted through the hospital (I seem to remember being wheeled there, but it's all a bit fuzzy.), up an elevator, to a big set of plate glass doors. Signs on the door warned that the people inside could be a flight risk. I realized that was about to mean me. My mind swirled around the term. I imagined myself and a whole troop of my fellow patients flying away from the hospital, the employees in awe of our telekinetic prowess. My imagination was in a weird sort of hyperdrive, perhaps to create a layer of denial between my mind and the fact that those big, glass doors would soon be locking behind me.

The nurse went to a wall phone and dialed through. The big doors clicked unlocked. We went in. I signed in. Waited again. Then another nurse in white coat came and told my friend it was time to leave. He departed with a few encouraging words and promised to check back in the next day. The big doors locked behind him. I was inside. The nurse took me to a gently lit office—by this time it was night—and asked me the same standard bank of questions the social worker had posed in the ER. She was the picture of professionalism: completely non-anxious, not cold, but also not shocked by anything I said.

One of the standard questions, after, "Do you think you might try to hurt yourself?" is "Do you think you might want to hurt anyone else?" My mind latched on to one of the seemingly minor triggers that had come to loom so large in my destructive self-evaluation of the past week:

"I kind of want to murder Verizon customer service right now."

The nurse looked at me out of the side of her eyes. Her demeanor and language shifted, just for a moment, from the professional to the colloquial: "Honey," she said, "that just don't count."

You may have already noticed that the buffers and safety nets that saved me are simply not accessible to many people who struggle with disordered moods and mental health challenges. The number for a suicide hotline, a friend I can call who has some skill in navigating the tricky waters of mental breakdowns, a chaplain who understands mental illness as illness to be treated and not as weakness of faith simply to be prayed away, access to medical treatment—these are not resources that simply fall into the laps of everyone who needs them. The stigma and shame that has surrounded mental illness deters many people from getting the help they need; the brokenness of this country's health care system in general, and mental health care system in particular, prevents many others. These two factors—stigmatizing silence and economic barriers—inform and reinforce each other. How can we fix the mental health care system in this country without breaking the silence about mental illness? And yet, how can we break the silence without providing people support and access to resources for recovery?

It's a massive challenge, requiring a multi-layered response. Policy changes are needed. So are safe spaces to share stories, and individuals brave enough to share. So, too, are preventive measures. I am very grateful, for example, that I did not have easy access to a handgun during this time of my life, which meant that the pressing question of how I could end my life was a complex, rather than a lethally simple one, to answer. As it was, I found myself in a hospital bed, with cuts, scratches, and burns all over my left arm, cracking out of place jokes to the nurse intern and holding onto my cell phone like it was a flotation device, as if I had some inward sense, deeply buried, that connection was the only thing that could save me.

It took about eight hours between the moment I limped into Sibley and my actual admission into a bed in Ward 7 West, the psychiatric unit where I would spend the next two weeks. When I had emerged from the basement and informed one of my housemates that I was headed to the hospital, she had the forethought to make me eat. It was the only meal I had that day. It would be a day before anyone could bring me clothes; somehow, I had thought to bring a phone charger. There was something fitting about that first night in the hospital, stripped of most possessions, even my shoelaces, wearing nothing but boxers, a hospital robe, and bright blue hospital socks. It was as if all the armor and barricades that I had constructed between the tempest raging internally and my outside affect had been pulled away, revealing the cuts and burns on my naked arms and the exposed, vulnerable mess of my actual experience. The next day, I was put on psychiatric medication for the first time in my life. Something in that initial cocktail must have had an effect: I slept through the night for the first time in a week.

I won't share every moment of those two weeks at Sibley, nor recount in detail each subsequent hospitalization—three in all—before I was admitted into a longer-term program at a hospital in Connecticut. Hospital wards are characterized by boredom, and I wonder whether the desperate boredom of the psychiatric ward is a major obstacle to healing, or whether it is mental illness itself that breeds the tendency toward languor and ennui. My father, who suffers from a mood disorder, describes depression as a feeling of trying to walk through molasses. Sometime that first day I asked for a pen and a pad of paper, and I began to write obsessively. In hindsight, much of what I wrote during that time is incoherent, clearly manic, or simply wrathful, but there are occasional moments of lucidity. In one such moment, I stumbled into an image that would follow me over the next six months as I bounced in and out of four acute psychiatric hospitalizations, one outpatient program, and one transitional living program housed on a hospital campus. It was an image of Christ on the psych ward:

Hebrews 1:3 says that "[Jesus] is the reflection of God's glory, and the exact imprint of God's very being, and he sustains all things–bears along all things–by his powerful word."

Christ bears along. These words are giving me some comfort. The Human One who is the imprint among us of God's very being is the same One who bears all things with us, who sustains us and holds us in being.

Christ is on the psych ward, bearing along. Suffering along. Sustaining the woman who can't sleep can't sleep can't sleep. Bearing along the scared young person with the addiction who wants to stop hating herself, wants to stop being disgusted with herself. Suffering with all those who feel they break relationship, hurt people, want to hurt themselves.

This Jesus knows a thing or two about broken relationships, about people hurting, about a body tearing itself apart. "Because he himself was tested by what he suffered, he is able to help those who are being tested" (Heb. 2:18). "All this is from God, who reconciled us to himself through Christ, and has given us the ministry of reconciliation" (2 Cor. 5:18). And this reconciliation, this bearing along, has a universality to it, for it is Christ "through whom [God] also created the world" (Heb. 1:2) and "in him all things in heaven and on earth were created" (Col 1:16) and are held together (Col. 1:17).

So here is Christ on the psych ward, just like Christ at the checkpoint or the food line or the refugee camp—bearing along, sustaining, holding together the jagged bits that cut, that bleed, to hold onto.

"I'm not going to lie to you. I feel really awkward, but I'm glad I'm here," said one visitor. "I might be a mess, but I'll be there," said another. "Solidarity is salvation," said a third. Here are people who, whether they know it or not, are bearers of the Christ who bears along all things, sustains all things. The one who sits with, the one who listens, who bears up, who holds your hand or your arm when you thought all it could hold was the knife of self-injury; they merge, somehow, mysteriously, sacramentally, into the One who ultimately holds us together at the most broken place of all.

Life. Death. Resurrection.

Christ is here on the psych ward as surely as in any book or any church. "What matters is you getting better," the social workers say. "What matters is your healing." But they also say, "Some of the best insights come from each other," or, "does anyone else in the group resonate with what _____ just said?"

"I feel so fragile." "I just wish I could sleep." "I'm embarrassed, ashamed."

Lord Jesus Christ, Son of God, Savior, be gracious to us.

We are your broken ones.

The months following that journal entry were marked by feelings of desperation, loneliness, confusion, and pain; and yet, somehow, I had some cognizance of the presence of Christ in the midst of the jagged shards of it all. I don't want to overly spiritualize my experience, nor romanticize mental illness. I also do not want to universalize my story, as if there is some easily traceable corollary between mental illness and religious experience. As I will insist in the next chapter, any discussion of God's presence must also make room for the experience or perception of God's absence. Yet a quick glance back at my journals during this time reminds me of how prayerful and reflective I was during this time—far more so, ironically, than I had been during my first year of seminary! What do I make of this paradoxical experience of God's presence in the midst of some of the most difficult months of my life? It was certainly not a "feeling" of God being with me—my feelings at the time were doing their best to kill me. With all respect to Horatio Spafford, it was not "well with my soul." I experienced feelings of abandonment and despair, misdirected anger and deep doubt. If God was present in it all, what sort of God could I possibly be talking about?

That's the question, as I look back over my time in various hospitals, that slowly emerged from the messiness and pain. What sort of God was I talking about? I, who pursued a seminary education, who spoke of a call to ministry, who aspired to serve the church. What sort of language could I find to describe this God? What is the shape of a faith in this God? The understanding of God that I found myself crawling into was not an omnipotent, omniscient, Wholly Other Being thundering from above—though in the summer storms that swept over Sibley, I did imagine the voice of God in the thunder. Nor was it a God who sent suffering as some sort of test or trial—though I certainly cried out in pain against such a God, against such a test, which, if it existed, I was convinced I was most certainly failing. No. In order to imagine God present with me on the psych ward, I found myself drawn to images of vulnerability, even weakness. Images of a God who draws close to human suffering, even submitting God's own self to suffering. A God intimately familiar with the pain and contradictions not only of the human condition in general, but also the particularities of harmful experiences.

Perhaps I had been introduced to this image of God bit by bit over the course of my life. Perhaps some intuition about this God had kept me close to the Christian tradition where, I

now believe, such an understanding of God is in fact very familiar, even if it is often covered over by neo-Platonic understandings of the Divine as the Unmoved Mover. Perhaps I was simply
grasping at straws. Regardless, it is where I find myself now,
with an understanding or intuition of God as the vulnerable
one, the hurting one, who suffers with those whose suffering is
too great to bear.

It would be a mischaracterization to say that my understanding of God saved me during those months of suffering.
I wasn't saved by an intellectual understanding or an image.
I was saved by specific people and concrete things, by friends
and family, by faith communities and counselors, by safe hospitals and medications. I came to understand the presence of
God in and among all of those particular people and things,
and, on reflection, realized that this type of divine presence
called for different understandings and images than those that
have tended to dominate Western Christian discourse. In the
same way, I won't argue that a particular understanding of God,
a particular theological vocabulary, is what's needed to save
the church. There are all sorts of concrete changes needed to
see the church through the challenges it faces over the next
decades. What all those concrete changes have in common,
however, is a fundamental shift in our understanding of God,
God's power, and God's activity in the world. There are, and
will always be, all sorts of things that need to be done, but it
has become my sense that the types of things that need to be
done only make sense as faithful responses in the light of a vulnerable God: a God of solidarity rather than distance, a God of
seeming weakness rather than overt power—the God whom I
found, almost by accident, hidden on the psych ward.

Fortunately for us, then, we do not have to go far to find such an
understanding of God. This vulnerable God, who acts in solidarity with human suffering and weakness, is present throughout

our scriptures. Theologian William Placher employs the phrase "narratives of a vulnerable God" to refer to the Christian scriptures, and writes of the ways in which these narratives subvert commonly held notions of the divine:

> Most people, in cultures where Christianity has been a dominant religious influence, assume that they know roughly what the word "God" means. Whether or not they believe in God, whether or not they find God an attractive notion they do have an idea of God, an idea that tends to center on power. . . . The Christian gospel, however, starts its understanding of God from a very different place. To read the biblical narratives is to encounter a God who is, first of all, love (1 John 4:8). Love involves a willingness to put oneself at risk, and God is in fact vulnerable in love, vulnerable even to great suffering.[1]

It was perhaps some inkling of this divine vulnerability, and its expression in solidarity with suffering humanity, that drew my eye to the passages in Hebrews and Colossians as I wrote in my journal about Christ present on the psych ward. In Hebrews, Christ is "the Son, whom God appointed heir of all things, through whom God also created the worlds. He is the reflection of God's glory and the exact imprint of God's very being" (Heb. 1:2–3a). Christ, according to the letter to the Colossians, is "the image of the invisible God, the firstborn of all creation; for in him all things in heaven and on earth were created, things visible and invisible, whether thrones or dominions or rulers or powers—all things have been created through him and for him. He himself is before all things, and in him all things hold together" (Col. 1:15–17). And of course, the prologue of the Fourth Gospel speaks of Jesus as the incarnate Word, who "was in the beginning with God" and through whom "all things came into being" (John 1:2–3).

In all three of these passages the authors are not content merely to make an ontological claim—that the world was created through Christ—but, instead, link that claim to Christ's activity of solidarity. Perhaps most formatively for the Christian tradition, John's Gospel proclaims that the Word through which all things came into being "became flesh and lived among us," becoming vulnerable in order to bridge the alienation between Creator and creation (John 1:14). The author of Hebrews continues their reflection on Christ and creation by stating that Christ "sustains all things by his powerful word" (Heb. 1:3b). The word "sustains" can also be translated "bears along" or "carries." Christ "bears along" in solidarity with the pain of creation and humanity. It was this "bearing along" that leapt off the page and into my heart as I sat in my bed on the psych ward. Bearing along—that is exactly what I needed Jesus to do. The author of Colossians adds that "through him God was pleased to reconcile to himself all things, whether on earth or in heaven, by making peace through the blood of his cross" (Col. 1:20). The suffering of Jesus on the Cross, in solidarity with suffering humanity, is not simply a material event but also, somehow, brings about the cosmic reunification of alienated humanity with God. German theologian Jürgen Moltmann writes that, "Jesus therefore dies the death of everything that lives in solidarity with the whole sighing creation."[2]

Such language about the Cross brings us into the realm of atonement theology. Yet the atonement language that has risen to prominence in the American church, often referred to as penal substitutionary atonement, is as far from Christ on the psych ward as one can get. From its bizarre splitting of the Trinity, to the strange dichotomy it creates between God's justice and God's mercy, to the observation made by feminist and womanist theologians that it not only glorifies suffering but glorifies child abuse, penal substitutionary atonement seems like bad news for people with mental health struggles. The idea that humanity's irredeemable sinfulness and guilt can only be forgiven through a wrathful Father violently sacrificing his Son (the gendered language here is quite intentional) sounds less like good news for those suffering and is, instead, the kind of disturbing, intrusive image that might lead one to the psych ward in the first place. One fellow-sufferer at Sibley, after seeing me reading my Bible, asked me with great sincerity whether I thought she was the sacrificial lamb meant for slaughter. To this, I would hope Christian theology could reply, "No, God is not like that," rather than, "No, you would be except that Jesus was already slaughtered for you, so that's over and done with."

On the Cross—and indeed, through his whole life and through the resurrection—Jesus makes the powerful statement: "No, God is not like that." God does not stand over and against suffering humanity as a condemning force of violence. God, through Jesus Christ, by the power of the Holy Spirit, is bearing along with humanity. Suffering along. Atoning—the word means, quite simply, "at-one-ing," making at one, unifying—by virtue of overcoming and undermining isolation, alienation, separation. Jesus "makes peace by the blood of his cross," not because his death is some sort of magical transactional exchange which satisfies an otherwise wrathful God, but because Christ's presence on the Cross is the presence of God at the very center of suffering, making peace in places where there seems to be no hope for peace—including, I pray, in the troubled minds of those of us who have spent long hours on the psych ward, feeling isolated, lonely, and afraid, and wondering where God could be found. "Right here," Jesus says at the Cross. "I can be found right here."

Our scriptures, of course, are multi-vocal. For every passage I cite to paint an image of God's vulnerable solidarity, there are other passages that picture God as warrior, as conquering king, or as angry father. I have no interest in denying either the existence or the power of those images. Rather, underneath the thundering voice of these images, I want us to recover a quieter, sometimes even a whispering, counter-voice. Somehow, it was that quiet voice that I could finally manage to hear underneath the noise of my mental illness. And I believe it is only that quiet voice that will be able to whisper, to breathe, fresh life into our calling as individuals and communities.

Christ is on the psych ward, bearing along. And the same Christ who found me there in the hospital is found everywhere that we, as individuals and as a church, are called to be. There is not one Christ for those with mental illness and another for the rest of the world. There is one Christ for all. There is not one church or one ministry for those with mental illness and another for the rest of the world. There is one church for all. While the ministry of Christian community will always look different in different contexts and different places, if we are truly to live into our identity as the Body of Christ, then the type of body we will be is a vulnerable one. This is a scary truth, but it might just be the truth that saves us. All of us. For we are God's broken ones.

Notes

1. William C. Placher, *Narratives of a Vulnerable God: Christ, Theology, and Scripture* (Louisville, KY: Westminster John Knox, 1994), xiii.

2. Jürgen Moltmann, *The Way of Jesus Christ* (Minneapolis: Fortress Press, 1993), 170.

2

A Deep and Terrifying Darkness

The first time I was hospitalized, I was scared. I had no idea what was about to happen, what it meant, or where I would go from there. It was a confusing and disorienting experience, a shattering of my own notion of myself. It was frightening.

The second time I was hospitalized, I was angry. I was angry at myself for landing back in the hospital. I was angry at the hospital for not curing me. I was angry at the world, at God, at my psych ward roommate, at anyone or anything onto which I could project my rage. I remember trying to write about how I felt, stabbing at a yellow legal pad with a pen until the anger bubbled over with more force than either pen or page could handle. I threw both across the room.

The third time, I felt nothing except a bottomless sense of despair. The Sibley Hospital psychiatric ward was starting to be familiar. Not comforting familiar, though. Trapped-here-forever familiar. There might not be any way out of this familiar. I stopped wondering whether I would ever feel better and started assuming I wouldn't.

Soon after I was released from my first hospitalization, I shared the "Christ on the Psych Ward" journal entry on my personal blog. It captured something important, I thought, something worth sharing. The next day, I wrote a follow-up post to make sure people understood that most of what I had written while on the psych ward was neither eloquent nor elegant. I wanted people to know my experience was mainly painful and disjointed and scary. I wanted people to know that mental illness really, really sucked.

That old blog site has long since expired, but the sentiment bears repeating: any eloquent description of the experience of mental health struggle conceals as much as it reveals. In particular, words conceal the incoherence, the indescribable reality, of mental illness. Words about anything difficult can have the unintended consequence of making that thing seem easier to manage, and it is the unmanageability of the thing that needs to be communicated, if only in order to clarify and contextualize the challenges of managing it. If you really want to understand words about mental illness, you first have to come up against, and let yourself fully experience, the failure of words. If you want truly to understand the radical nature of God's presence, which I believe is the gospel message, you first have to come up against, and let yourself fully experience, the absence of God. The failure of God.

Isn't this a heretical claim, not only in terms of a traditional Christian understanding, but also in terms of the very understanding of God I explored in the last chapter? The dozens of journals in which I recorded my experience are full to bursting, but many of the entries seem unfit for a book on Christian spirituality. They are shards of anger—even hate; they are pages of profanity, shrapnel from the explosion of my self-image. As it turns out, however, such shards are not foreign to the Christian spiritual tradition, but are central to it. The narrative of hope and resurrection on which the faith of so many rests is inseparable from stories of despair and crucifixion. In biblical terms, these stories employ the language of lament.

The book of Psalms is the prayer book of the Bible. There is no parallel collection of literature in the New Testament; it would take the Church centuries to come up with its own prayer books, and, even then, those collections drew heavily on the ancient Hebrew psalms. If my experiences with mental illness have affirmed God's presence even in, and especially in, places of hurt and brokenness—the presence of Christ on the psych ward—it is only because they have also brought me face-to-face with the very real possibility of God's absence. Though such a statement might seem blasphemous, it is deeply biblical. The Psalms, and the surrounding literature of the Jewish and Christian scriptures, are shot through with language of God's absence. Again and again, the psalmists cry out to God to return to them, to remember them, to make God's self visible to them: "Why, O LORD, do you stand far off? Why do you hide yourself in times of trouble?" (Psalm 10:1) But if God is present everywhere, how could God ever stand far off or hide? How could God go missing?

"My soul thirsts for God, for the living God. When shall I come and behold the face of God? My tears have been my food day and night, while people say to me continually, 'Where is your God?'" (Psalm 42:2–3) Can God forget? Shouldn't the answer to the taunting question, "Where is your God?" be quite simple to answer? After all, God is everywhere!

"O God, you have rejected us, broken our defenses; you have been angry; now restore us!" (Psalm 60:1) Is God this fickle, getting angry and rejecting people and then restoring them to relationship because they ask nicely?

"O LORD, why do you cast me off? Why do you hide your face from me? Wretched and close to death from my youth up, I suffer your terrors; I am desperate. Your wrath has swept over me; your dread assaults destroy me. They surround me like a flood all day long; from all sides they close in on me. You have caused friend and neighbor to shun me; my companions are in darkness" (Psalm 88:14–18). Does God cast people off? Hide from them? Destroy them with wrathful attacks? How could such a God be present in vulnerability and solidarity?

"Hear my prayer, O LORD; let my cry come to you. Do not hide your face from me in the day of my distress. Incline your ear to me; answer me speedily in the day when I call" (Psalm

102). And, perhaps most famously of all within the Christian appropriation of these ancient Jewish prayers (which we will return to, in more detail, in a moment):

"My God, my God, why have you forsaken me? Why are you so far from helping me, from the words of my groaning? O my God, I cry by day, but you do not answer; and by night, but find no rest" (Psalm 22:1–2).

The language of these and many other psalms—language echoed throughout the biblical tradition—is only coherent if it emerges from experiences of God's departure, God's forgetting, God's absence.

To be sure, the psalmists, like other biblical authors and redactors, are not offering carefully crafted, systematic understandings of theology. They are speaking out of experiences of pain and hurt. In order to understand them, in order actually to get inside the language of scripture, we must not move too quickly to the "but" of the psalmist. "Yet you are holy, enthroned on the praises of Israel," the author of Psalm 22 writes after they write of feeling forsaken; "But you, O LORD, are enthroned forever," sings Psalm 102. This literature comes after experience, after reflection. The experience itself does not resolve so quickly. That the psalms, among other voices within the biblical canon, give voice to such experiences is an affirmation of the importance of acknowledging them.

Such affirmation is not always to be found in Christian circles, however. It is certainly lacking in the sort of "positive thinking" faith espoused by prosperity gospel preachers and quoted on the various pastel goods for sale at many a Christian book store. But other strands of Christian thought are suspicious of the centering of any kind of human experience. In her book *Darkness Is My Only Companion*—the title itself taken from the language of Psalm 88—Episcopal priest Kathryn Greene-McCreight shares her own grappling with faith and scripture in the midst of mental illness. She discusses the effect mental illness has on a person's sense of personality and feeling:

What does this mean before God that the personality should seem to dry up and be born away on the wind? I suppose it means that the personality is relatively unimportant vis-à-vis God. In God's eyes we are not defined by how we feel, by what we think, even by what we do. . . . Of course, saying that personality is not very important is not acceptable in much of the Christian world these days, to say the least.[1]

Greene-McCreight critiques the modern Christian focus on feeling and experience, linking it to the rise of liberal theology:

In fact, feeling is not really that important for the life of faith. Ever since Friedrich Schleiermacher (1768–1834) defined religion as the feeling of absolute dependence, Christians in the Protestant West have tended to follow suit. Religion is often framed in terms of feeling and experience. . . . If we really thought that feeling is the essence of the Christian faith, the depressed Christian would be given all the more ammunition for self-destruction.[2]

I want to tread lightly here, in part because I affirm her underlying point: it is God's regard for us and action on our behalf, rather than our feelings, that are salvific, and in part because, just like me, she is speaking out of the depths of her own personal encounter with suffering. It is also the case, as friends and counselors reminded me during my darkest hours, that "feelings aren't facts." I find myself disagreeing, however, with her contention that feelings, while perhaps important for therapy, are unimportant in matters of faith. "I am simply questioning the religious significance of feelings," she writes, "especially for the Christian religion, in the economy of salvation. Our salvation is something Jesus wrought on the cross, not in the interiority of our personality."[3]

Yet, the very psalms from whom Greene-McCreight draws the title of her book and whose words occupy a prominent place in her text, are interested in both the economy of salvation and in feelings and experience. The two are, perhaps, not as separate as all that—not because God somehow loves us less when we are feeling crushed or are unable to feel at all, but because God's love is active in the middle of our messy, fractured lives with all of our personality flaws and emotional dysregulation. Feelings aren't facts, it's true, but they are part of who we are, and so they are part of what God loves when God loves us. The psalms, as the fourth-century theologian and articulator of Christian orthodoxy Athanasius comments, serve as a mirror to the soul: "They show us a full range of human experiences, both beautiful and ugly."[4]

The psalmists, of course, have much to say in praise of God and God's sovereignty; they also have much to say about the challenges of the human experience and the times when divine power seems, somehow, to come up short. God's absence is as present in the Psalms as God's power. Only by taking that absence seriously can the true power of the psalms—and thus, the true power of God—be fully appreciated. Perhaps that it is why, again and again throughout my mental health struggles, I have turned to the words of the psalmists. The best description of my own painful experience comes, not from a psychiatrist's handbook, but from the ancient words of Psalm 102:

> Hear my prayer, O Lord;
>   let my cry come to you.
> Do not hide your face from me
>   in the day of my distress.
> Incline your ear to me;
>   answer me speedily in the day when I call.
> For my days pass away like smoke,
>   and my bones burn like a furnace.

My heart is stricken and withered like grass;
    I am too wasted to eat my bread.
Because of my loud groaning
    my bones cling to my skin.
I am like an owl of the wilderness,
    like a little owl of the waste places.
I lie awake;
    I am like a lonely bird on the housetop.
All day long my enemies taunt me;
    those who deride me use my name for a curse.
For I eat ashes like bread,
    and mingle tears with my drink,
because of your indignation and anger;
    for you have lifted me up and thrown me aside.
My days are like an evening shadow;
    I wither away like grass.
But you, O Lord, are enthroned forever;
    your name endures to all generations.
You will rise up and have compassion on Zion,
    for it is time to favor it;
    the appointed time has come.
For your servants hold its stones dear,
    and have pity on its dust. (102:1–14)

This is the first half of the psalm. The psalmist stands before God, in the naked and vulnerable reality of his own experience, bringing nothing to God in prayer other than an honest account of his own suffering.

The second half deals with what Greene-McCreight might call "the economy of salvation":

Let this be recorded for a generation to come,
    so that a people yet unborn may praise the LORD:
that he looked down from his holy height,
    from heaven the LORD looked at the earth,

to hear the groans of the prisoners,
    to set free those who were doomed to die;
so that the name of the LORD may be declared in Zion,
    and his praise in Jerusalem,
when peoples gather together,
    and kingdoms, to worship the LORD. (102:18–22)

The two are not separate. They are intertwined.

To understand why and how suffering and salvation are intertwined is to take a journey directly to the wounded heart of the Christian tradition—to the Cross of Jesus Christ, and beyond it to the empty tomb. Not surprisingly, at the Cross we hear the language of the Psalms. Jesus dies with the agonized words of the psalmist wrenched from his lips: "And about three o'clock Jesus cried out with a loud voice, 'Eli, Eli, lema sabachthani?' that is, 'My God, my God, why have you forsaken me?'" (Psalm 22:1; Matthew 27:46; Mark 15:34) Irish theologian Peter Rollins points out the significance of Matthew's account of Jesus crying out, not in Hebrew or the Greek of the Septuagint, but in his native Aramaic:

> In the Jewish faith, the Hebrew Scriptures are read, memorized, and recalled in the original language, not one's native tongue, so while this cry might be inspired by the psalm, the words reflect a person's heartfelt cry of agony. . . . We must . . . give this cry its full theological and existential weight. We must read it with all of its horror and potency. It is a cry that comes from one cut off from all grounding in a deeper reality, one who has lost all sense of meaning, all mythological frames. It is a cry that exposes us to a man utterly destitute. Here, right at the heart of Christianity, God despairs of God.[5]

God despairs of God. The mind and heart reels at the thought. German theologian Jürgen Moltmann refers to this scene as "the Godforsakenness of the Son of God."[6]

For Kathryn Greene-McCreight, the emotional suffering associated with mental illness makes it good news that salvation is an event outside of the personality: "Our salvation is something Jesus wrought on the cross, not in the interiority of our personality."[7] When I look to the Cross, however, and I see the Godforsakenness of God's Child—when I see God despairing of God—I see a powerful solidarity with the anguish my personality experiences in the depths of mental and emotional strife. The Cross of Christ exposes a horrifying interiority. Jesus cries out, wondering aloud whether he has been abandoned by God . . . and there is no answer. The heavens are silent. We do not hear God's voice—which emerged from a cloud just a few chapters before—respond to Jesus' cry. There is only silence. The contradiction of the moment is not resolved for us, the observers and readers.

Today, we have the luxury of reading of Jesus's agony in the context of the Resurrection. But pause, here, for a moment. Pause here with the disciples, with the women at the foot of the cross, and apparently, with Jesus himself; pause, not knowing the answer to Jesus' question. Has God truly abandoned Jesus? If we believe Jesus is divine, has God abandoned even God's self? Is God entirely absent at the Cross? We have no answers. Only silence.

For some, the idea of God's absence at the Cross has been transformed into a theology of atonement I find problematic. For this group, God abandons Jesus on the Cross because God cannot look upon sin, and Jesus, on the Cross, is taking on the sins of the world. The passage often cited to back up this claim is the wildly out-of-context Habakkuk 1:13: "Your eyes are too pure to behold evil, and you cannot look on wrongdoing." Read the rest of the verse, and we have exactly the kind of crying out in lament of the absence of God I have been addressing: "Why do you look on the treacherous, and are silent when the wicked swallow those more righteous than they?" God's absence is not some piece of the systematic theology puzzle, nor an ingredient in a bloody magic trick that conjures away human sin. Chapter 3 will deal more directly with questions of sin and separation; for now, suffice it to say that biblical texts about the absence of God emerge from painful human experience as cries of protest in the face of suffering and evil.

My encounter with the self-directed violence that emerged from the "interiority of my personality," as Greene-McCrieght phrases it, brought me face to face with the question of God's silence. God's absence. What is most difficult to explain but what I most wish to be able to communicate is that I am not speaking about an intellectual doubt here, but something deeper and more tortured. There were times in the hospital when I was despairing of or doubting the existence of God in the midst of my pain. Had visitors shared their intellectual or even their initial emotional responses, they would have gone unheard. "But David," people could have said, "God is always with you, even in this difficult time." Perhaps some did say that. And perhaps, from a theological standpoint, their statements would have been true. But, from within the storm of mental illness, I could not always hear that truth. Just as, when I shared that I felt lonely, isolated, and abandoned, I could not hear the truth of the very people who were there with me, saying, "We are here. We have not abandoned you." I could not internalize that truth in the midst of my pain. I remember relatively little of what anyone *said* to me while I was in the hospital, yet, years later, I absolutely remember who was there.

In the hospital, I needed the presence of people. People with bodies. Those people were able to provide presence, paradoxically, by being willing and able to sit with the discomfort of my expressions of abandonment and isolation. I didn't need disembodied, intellectual arguments about God's presence. I needed people who could be physically and emotionally present when I asked, "Why isn't God present?" In those people, and in my experience of absence, I experienced God's presence by questioning God's presence.

It is difficult for me to share a single story that captures the experience. In part, because my experience is so far beyond words. In part, because my time in and out of the hospital cannot be neatly divided into "times I experienced God as present" and "times I experienced God as absent." The experiences weave in and out of each other, inform each other, shape each other. To encounter God in the crying out against the absence of God is not an easy reality to name. The title of this chapter is taken from the story of God's covenant with Abram in Genesis 15. Both the story and the phrase "a deep and terrifying darkness" are, for me, a powerful summation of the fragmented and often terrifying experience of mental illness; they also speak to any encounter with suffering which raises questions about the existence of a good God.

In theological parlance, a revelation of God's presence is called a theophany. Theophanies, in scripture, are often accompanied by signs of God's power over creation: fire, lightning, thunder, earthquake; blinding light knocking Saul to the ground. God shows up and those who experience the theophany know, beyond a shadow of a doubt, that God is there. God makes God's self known in a dramatic way. When I want to hear from God, I want that kind of encounter. I could do without the earthquakes, but I want the certainty—the convincing evidence that God is here, that God has something to say directly to me. When I cry out, "God, why have you abandoned me?" I am hoping to receive a flamboyant theophany in response.

Genesis 15 is the story of a theophany, but it challenges my expectations about what it means to encounter God. This is a central story in the Hebrew Bible: the first covenant with Abram. God, having called Abram from his home into a strange country, promises him descendants and land. It is quite a promise for an old man with no children, wandering landless. The story foreshadows all that is to come—the birth of the Israelite nation, the captivity in Egypt, the Exodus, the violent entry into the "Promised Land."[8] I don't think it's an exaggeration to say that without this story the rest of the Hebrew Bible doesn't make much sense. That said, I am fascinated by how ambiguous, even fractured, the story is, how caught up in fear and darkness. It's a story about a promise, but it's an uncertain and uncomfortable one.

I want to point out a few things about this text. The covenant ceremony described is one the first hearers and readers of this text would have known but which we, in the twenty-first century, are unfamiliar with. The description of the ceremony is remarkably detailed considering the usually sparse nature of biblical narratives. We are given a list of the animals involved and a description of the process of preparing them and protecting them from scavengers. The sacrifices are then accepted by God in a haunting scene involving "a smoking fire pot and a flaming torch." What is going on? The way we translate from the Hebrew sheds some light. The Common English Bible translates, "That day the LORD *cut* a covenant with Abram" (Gen 15:18). The Inclusive Bible expands on the reason behind this translation: "In Hebrew, the word 'covenant' is derived from the verb 'to cut.' Usually both parties cut the sacrifice jointly, as if to say, 'May this happen to me if I violate our agreement.'"[9] When Abram asks, "How am I to know that I shall possess [the land]" (v.8), God responds with a radical commitment, saying, in effect, "If I don't hold up my end of this deal, I am going to get cut. I am going to be hurt." This is a vulnerable God. A God who exposes God's self to risk and to pain.

What brings about this radical commitment from God? Abram's doubt. Throughout this passage Abram challenges God, asks God pointed questions, wonders how he can possibly know that God is serious about the promise. Abram is often lifted up as a paragon of faith, as one who does what God tells him to do. And here he is, doubting, and forcing a response—a radical response, a vulnerable response—from God. The promise is wrapped up in doubt, and the doubt doesn't manifest itself only in the form of Abram's questions. The whole passage is fractured and caught up in darkness. When God first addresses Abram, God tells him to go out and count the stars—it must be nighttime. God talks to Abram some more,

and we are told that the sun is going down. Did a whole night
and day go by here, or is the story out of order? Then it's nighttime again and we get a spooky scene with a smoking pot and a
flaming torch. Time is fluid in this passage. It is fragmented—
like experiences of trauma and suffering. Trauma disrupts our
sense of time, makes seconds last hours and days disappear
like smoke. The story moves from nighttime to the sun going
down to "a deep sleep fell upon Abram, and a deep and terrifying darkness descended upon him" (v.12). I can't get rid
of that line. It sticks in my heart. A deep and terrifying darkness. That's what I feel when I read news about violence in the
world, when I hear stories of oppression, suffering, or abuse.
That's what I feel when mental illness swirls around me and I
have what we clinically call a "depressive episode" and my brain
is trying to kill me. A deep and terrifying darkness.

Abram encounters God in a fragmented way, and in a deep
and terrifying darkness, which tells us something about how
we encounter God. This story from Genesis is almost a reverse
theophany. It does not happen with a thundering voice or
with beams of light. It takes place under deep and terrifying
darkness. It is in darkness and confusion that God—a radically
committed God, a vulnerable God—shows up. It is an uncomfortable place to be. A scary place. A place where there are no
easy answers, where, in fact, there might not be any answers
at all. It is not the place where we expect to find God. It is a
place where we might describe our experience as the absence
of God. We cannot, however, be so quick to leave this place, for
God is present exactly in the absence.

Please don't mistake my meaning. I do not like the deep and
terrifying darkness. I like sunshine. I like clarity. I like answers
and certainty. What I encounter in this passage is faith, Abram's
exemplary faith, expressed through doubt. I encounter a sense
of time that does not march by mechanically, but ebbs and
flows chaotically. I encounter promises made in darkness, cove-
nants cut in haunting scenes, God's presence as absence. What

seems like bad news—doubt, fragmentation, darkness—is actually good news. The doubt and darkness match our experiences, and we can only meet God in and through our experiences. We can only encounter God—the God who heals—if we are willing to stay with the hurt, to experience it. If we are not willing to stay, for awhile, in the deep and terrifying darkness, then we are going to have a hard time following the Jesus, the Christ, about whom we sing and to whom we pray. For even when the disciples encounter Jesus after the Resurrection, they find that he still bears the scars of his torture and death. Our trauma does not simply disappear. It remains. The deep and terrifying darkness is not simply gone, but there is a word in that darkness, a further word of radical commitment and vulnerability.

Today's Church needs to relearn how to stay in the deep and terrifying darkness, and we need to do so in multiple venues. In pastoral care, we must develop a comfort for sitting in discomfort, for standing in solidarity with those who cry out from an experience of God's absence, without correcting or cajoling. In missions and social justice, we must open ourselves up to "being cut," as God does in Genesis 15, which means committing ourselves to listening to the voices of communities who feel abandoned, including communities that have historically been abandoned and hurt by the church, even as the people in those communities criticize us or speak out in anger toward us. In worship, we must learn to reclaim the language of the psalmists and open up space for communal lament. Citing studies on the absence of lament in the hymnody of U.S. churches, both mainline and evangelical, theologian Soong-Chan Rah writes:

> The American church avoids lament. The power of lament is minimized and the underlying narrative of suffering that requires lament is lost. But absence doesn't make the heart grow fonder. Absence makes the heart forget. The absence of lament in the liturgy of the American church results in the loss of memory. We forget the necessity of lamenting over suffering and pain. We forget the reality of suffering and pain.[10]

In Psalm 102, the psalmist cries out:

Hear my prayer, O Lord; let my cry come to you. Do not hide your face from me in the day of my distress.

Even when the psalm turns toward praise, the reality of suffering and trauma does not simply disappear:

But you, O Lord, are enthroned forever; your name endures to all generations. You will rise up and have compassion on Zion, for it is time to favor it; the appointed time has come. For your servants hold its stones dear, and have pity on its dust.

The Church, as God's servant, is called to have compassion for those who are suffering, those who feel abandoned by God. We are to hold dear those places in people's lives that seem to be ruined, reduced to rubble and stone. For the Church to be the Church, it must be a people who have pity even on the dust, who are present, in other words, in the midst of absence.

Notes

1. Kathryn Greene-McCreight, *Darkness Is My Only Companion: A Christian Response to Mental Illness,* 2nd ed. (Grand Rapids, MI: Brazos Press, 2015), 85.

2. Ibid., 90.

3. Ibid., 91.

4. Toni Craven and Walter Harrelson, "Excursus: Beauty," in *The New Interpreter's Study Bible: New Revised Standard Version with the Apocrypha* (Nashville, TN: Abingdon, 2003), 892.

5. Peter Rollins, *Insurrection* (New York: Howard Books, 2011), Kindle edition, chapter 2, location 425.

6. Jürgen Moltmann, *The Way of Jesus Christ* (Minneapolis: Fortress Press, 1993), 165–66.

7. Ibid., 91.

8. While this topic is beyond the scope of my book, the violence foreshadowed by the passage is problematic, particularly for indigenous populations. For one critique from a Palestinian Christian theologian, see Naim Stifan Ateek, *Justice and Only Justice: A Palestinian Theology of Liberation* (Maryknoll, NY: Orbis, 1989).

9. *The Inclusive Bible: The First Egalitarian Translation* (Lanham, MD: Sheed and Ward, 2007), 12.

10. Soong-Chan Rah, *Prophetic Lament: A Call for Justice in Troubled Times* (Downers Grove, IL: IVP Books, 2015), 22.

3

Who Told Us We Were Naked?

t is probably a terrible idea to dedicate a whole chapter of a book about mental illness to the topic of sin. There are all sorts of reasons to avoid the topic altogether, and all sorts of other reasons to limit my comments to the following: People do not suffer from mental health problems because of sin or lack of faith. Period. So that settles that, and we can now safely move on to the next chapter about the much nicer topic of grace.

Far too often, faith communities have enforced, rather than resisted, shame and stigma around mental health problems. In response to the harm done by such theologizing of people's despair, the obvious compassionate response is radically to disassociate sin from mental health problems. For the person who has heard stigmatizing messages about mental illness from their faith community, this is an important first step. When a sufferer asks, "Is God making me suffer because of my sin?," an appropriate response is, "Absolutely not!" If you are someone who has been the target of shame and stigma at the hands of a church or community that told you your suffering and your inability to experience joy are somehow your fault; if you have done, or are doing, the difficult work of unlearning those deeply wounding messages; if what you need to hear right now, and tomorrow, and the next day, is, "This is not your fault," then let me say it to you: "This is not your fault."

It's not. There's nothing more broken about you than there is about any of the rest of us. If that's what you need to hear, then hear it now, and be done with the thing. There's no need to dig through any of the rest of my ramblings on the topic.

Nevertheless, there is something about this topic that compels me to ramble. For one thing, the suffering of mental illness is exacerbated by stigma and a maze of barriers to care that are worthy of condemnation as societal sins. Stigma causes real harm. It prevents people from asking for help. It tells lies, spreads misinformation. Much of Jesus's life can be understood as an entering into relationship with those most stigmatized in his society. Jesus's ministry can be read as a response to the sin of stigma. The stigma surrounding mental illness also intersects with other forms of oppression and societal injustice. In the U.S., a history of deinstitutionalization has led to high rates of homelessness and incarceration among people with severe mental illness. Furthermore, access to the care that exists is often limited by factors such as race, class, and identity. Theologian Robyn Henderson-Espinoza recounts their own experience of diagnosis and access:

> In 2009, I was diagnosed with a mental illness. As a nonbinary trans person of color, my Latinx heritage and family of origin did not school me in ways to access health care. But I was then-partnered with a cis white woman who worked in health care and knew how to navigate the hospital, so I received access to the best health care in Chicago. . . . I was dependent on my white cis partner to not only help me but advocate for me, and my treatment was all due to my cis white partner knowing how to navigate the health care system. Whiteness enabled me to have access to mental health care. And I was lucky.[1]

Societal sins of stigma, racism, heterosexism, and classism all factor in to the conversation about mental illness.

My own background also accounts for my reluctance to abandon entirely the conversation at the intersection of sin and mental illness. I did not come of age in a faith community that considered depression to be a result of sin. Mental illness was not spoken of as sinful in my home church because, as far as I can remember, it was not really spoken of at all. The stigma and shame of it was not overtly enforced, but rather silently assumed. When I found myself in the psych ward, my immediate assumption was not that I was being punished by God for my sins. I was, however, quite convinced that hospitalization represented a personal failure on my part. A stronger person, I reasoned (or un-reasoned, as the case might be) would have been able to hold it together. For some believers, the thought that depression is a form of divine punishment adds a horrifying layer of anxiety and pain to their experience. My reaction was almost the opposite. I fell quickly into what Parker Palmer has termed "functional atheism," or "the unconscious, unexamined conviction that if anything decent is going to happen here, we are the ones who must make it happen—a conviction held even by people who talk a good game about God."[2]

So while I did not associate my condition with sin exactly, I was very much consumed with shame. I struggled with the decision to let professors know about my condition in order to receive a medical withdrawal from classes. I delayed asking my parents to drive up from North Carolina. At one point, I spiraled down into a void of shame when I realized I would have to miss a friend's wedding because of hospitalization. I was also consumed with guilt or shame because of things I had said or done that had hurt people close to me. Sometimes it was the immediate past that was the focus of my obsessive guilt. At other times it was broken relationships or bad decisions in the more distant past, whether the past six months or the past twenty years. While the obsessive shame was certainly not healthy, the guilt was not always unwarranted. As someone who has been both a sufferer of mental illness and also a family member of someone who suffers, I know that people in the throes of a mental health crisis are not always easy to get along with, and can sometimes say or do hurtful things. I was now faced with the realization that *I* had been the one saying and doing hurtful things.

My suffering wasn't a punishment for my misdeeds; in fact, my mental health problems were probably at the root of many of the behaviors I felt so guilty for, not the other way around. Nevertheless, (and much to my own frustration) the connections between shame, and sin, and stigma, once examined closely, are not so easily untied. It's not that I believe mental illness is a result of sin. It's that I think my mental health struggles gave me a deeper, more honest appreciation for the brokenness and alienation of the human experience. Rightly understood, the Christian language of sin and salvation is meant to speak exactly about the experience of brokenness and alienation.

The word "sin," like most of the Christian lexicon, has been used, misused, and abused in myriad ways over the centuries of the Church's existence, and yet, as Barbara Brown Taylor writes in her book *Speaking of Sin,* "Abandoning the language of sin will not make sin go away."[3] Instead, Brown Taylor advocates for a reclamation of the deep roots of the language of sin, in contrast to what she identifies as two modern tendencies. The first, which she associates with more liberal churches, replaces sin with sickness, a condition which is no fault of ours. The second, associated with more conservative churches, replaces sin with legal language, in which we are responsible for our misdeeds and deserving of judicial accountability. She argues that these metaphors, while powerful in their own right, are not entirely up to the task:

> My concern is that neither the language of medicine nor the language of law is an adequate substitute for the language of theology, which has more room in it for paradox than either of the other two. In the theological model, the basic human problem is not sickness or lawlessness but sin. It is something we experience both as a species and as individuals, in our existential angst and in our willful misbehavior. However we

run into it, we run into it as wrecked relationship: with God, with one another, with the whole created order. Sometimes we cause the wreckage and sometimes we are simply trapped in it. . . . [T]he essence of sin is not the violation of laws but the violation of relationships.[4]

The language of sin, according to Brown Taylor, speaks to the brokenness of human relationship, and the ensuing experience of isolation and disconnection. "Deep down in human existence," she writes, "there is an experience of being cut off from life. . . . For ages and ages, this experience has been called sin—deadly alienation from the source of all life."[5]

Wrecked relationships. Alienation from life. A fundamental brokenness. These are realities that I understand exactly through the lens of mental illness. That's not because mental illness is "a sin," but rather because my struggles with mental health have put me in deep touch with the brokenness and pain that is a universal reality of human existence. We who have mental illness are no more sinful than anyone else, but perhaps we are able to be a bit more honest with the problem. You see, we've had a direct, personal encounter with the fragmentation and brokenness—the fear of isolation, alienation, and disconnection—that is at the root of the human experience we call "sin." Perhaps, then, it is worth examining what we're talking about when we talk about sin.

For centuries, Christian thought on the topic of sin has relied on a story that, despite its prominent place in theology and popular culture, is really rather odd. It involves a snake, and some fruit, and a God in the habit of taking evening strolls. I am speaking, of course, of Genesis 3, of the man and the woman who eat the fruit that God told them not to eat. Biblical scholar Susan Niditch points out that it is difficult to present fresh readings of this text: "All too often readers come to Genesis weighed down by Augustine's or Milton's interpretation of the story."[6] Yet a fresh reading of this text is essential in untying the threads of sin, shame, and suffering, and laying the groundwork for a destigmatizing theological understanding of mental health struggles. What if we were to read this strange story not as a story about disobedience or "The Fall," but rather as a story about broken relationship and alienation? About the harmful effects of shame on our human need for connection and belonging?

As it turns out, none of the Hebrew words that are usually translated into English as "sin," "transgression," or "iniquity" appear in the Genesis 3 account.[7] The text in its original form, or as close to its original form as we can get, is oddly devoid of the concept of "sin." The interrelated themes of nakedness and shame, on the other hand, play a central role in the narrative. "The man and his wife were both naked," we are told, "and were not ashamed" (Gen. 2:25). The stage is set with a depiction of two humans, innocent, unashamed, and most decidedly unclothed. Even the snake in the story is described as "naked," though this connection is often obscured by translation. The Inclusive Bible translation tries to capture the Hebrew segue: "Now, the woman and the man were *both naked*, though they were not ashamed. But the snake was *even more naked*: the most cunning of all the animals that YHWH had made."[8] The story actually starts with a pun: literally, the woman and the man are "smooth," but the snake is "smoother." By framing the story this way, the ancient narrators center nakedness as a key component. Whatever is about to happen next, it's going to have something to do with nudity and shame. This story establishes shame as an early, repeated motif in the Hebrew Bible.[9]

In their exploration of the relevance of Hebrew Bible texts for pastoral care and counseling, professors Denise Dombkowski Hopkins and Michael S. Koppel examine the role of shame: "Shame can be positive by helping us to maintain boundaries for appropriate behavior. Shame can also be negative in that it makes us feel deficient, flawed, and inferior—in short, not 'good enough.' Shame relates to who we are; guilt relates to what we do."[10] Echoing this analysis, social worker and researcher Brené Brown differentiates between guilt and shame.[11] Guilt, according to Brown, means I did something bad; shame means I am bad.[12] She defines shame as "the fear that something we've done or failed to do . . . makes us unworthy of connection. . . . Shame is the intensely personal feeling or experience of believing that we are flawed and there-fore unworthy of love and belonging."[13] Brown isn't speaking specifically about mental illness, but she might as well be tran-scribing my interior narrative as I admitted myself into the hospital for the first, second, and third times: "What if there is something irrevocably broken about me? What if the people who love and support me are wrong about me? What if I'm not worthy of love? What if I'm better off dead? What if the world is better off without me in it?"

If the nakedness of the woman and the man is linked to their being without shame, and shame is not the feeling that I have *done* something bad but rather that *I am bad*—somehow deficient or fundamentally flawed—then the character of the snake takes on a different dimension. Rather than the tempter of traditional interpretation, the snake is the voice of shame which points out deficiency: "God knows that when you eat of it your eyes will be opened, and you will be like God, knowing good and evil" (v.5). Once naked and unashamed, the woman now has a sense of lacking something, something that could be gained by eating the fruit of the tree. In modern terms, Brown refers to the "shame-based fear of being ordinary."[14] Interest-ingly, she observes that when humans experience shame, "we are almost always hijacked by the limbic system . . . that prim-itive fight-or-flight part of our brain."[15] The snake, then, stands in as an expression of our "reptilian brain" that takes over when shame kicks in—not bad or evil, necessarily, just primi-tive and reactionary, evolved for a different purpose than com-plex emotional interaction.[16]

Once the man and the woman have eaten from the fruit of the tree, the first thing they notice is their own nakedness, and their first act is to cover themselves. (v.7) No longer oblivious to their nakedness, they are also no longer unashamed. When they hear God taking a daily stroll through the garden, they hide, at which point, of course, God finds them and condemns them for their disobedience.

Well, not exactly. God's first words to the humans are not a condemnation, but a question: "Where are you?" (v.9) The open question gives the humans the ability to take responsibility for their actions or to share their feelings. Throughout the Hebrew Bible, humans have a particular response to being addressed by God. The word *hineini*, which means, "here I am," is uttered by priests, prophets, and patriarchs when God speaks their name. Responding with *hineini* can indicate "the ability to be present for and receptive to the other (Gen. 27:18), the readiness to act on behalf of another (Gen. 27:1), or the willingness to sacrifice for someone or something higher (Gen. 37:13)."[17] But the man in the garden does not say, "*Hineini.*"[18] Instead, his answer centers around the realization of nudity and fear—a newfound sense of what Brown calls "excruciating vulnerability."[19]

If the motif of nudity-shame is central to the story, then it is God's next question—"Who told you that you were naked?"—that serves as the turning point of the story, rather than the following question (v. 11) which, in many interpretations, takes center stage. Imagine God's tone of voice, not as that of an angry parent scolding disobedient children, but that of heartbreak over the damage shame causes. "Who told you," God's voice shakes, "that you were lacking in anything? Who told you that you were anything but beautiful and good?"

The question, "Who told us we were naked?" is of vital importance. What are the voices that tell us that we are lacking, that we are deficient, or that we should be ashamed and afraid? Who told me, as I sat in my dark apartment self-destructing, that I was worthless, that the world would be better off without me? There's not a single answer, or a single voice. There are a multitude of societal voices that whisper to us, of course, sending us

messages about the not-enough-ness of our bodies, our possessions, our lives. For me, I've come to understand mental illness
as one such voice, whose whispers I sometimes have to ignore,
sometimes engage, sometimes redirect. But that's not the whole
of it either, as the ancient story of the humans in the garden
reveals. There is something else, a—what? A primal wound, an
instinct, an original sin?—that whispers to us all. Jan Richardson, theologian and artist, tells a story that sums up the primor-
dial voice that whispers to us of our nakedness:

> In one of my earliest memories, I am perhaps five years old.
> I am standing in my parents' bedroom with a stack of my art-
> work. Drawings in pencil and crayon, paintings in tempera
> and watercolor and finger paint: these are the pieces that my
> mother has gathered up and saved. The entire collection.
> And I am systematically tearing up each one. The most vivid
> part of the memory is when my mother walks in. I have made
> it nearly to the bottom of the stack by this point. Horrified to
> see the pile of shredded paper, she asks me why I have done
> this. "Because they weren't any good!" I tell her, amazed that
> she can't see this for herself. I don't know where I got this
> idea; it didn't originate at home, where my family valued and
> supported creativity. Call it a precocious inner critic.[20]

"A precocious inner critic," is what Richardson calls this voice,
which she says did not come from critical parents or teachers.
There is a primal tendency we inherit as humans that predis-
poses us toward "they weren't any good." It's the whisper of the
snake—though the snake in the story is clever enough to dis-
guise the message, selling it as, "You could be like God." Why
settle, then, for just being loved?

It's remarkable to me how the centrality of nudity and
shame, once understood, unlocks this ancient story. Our ances-
tors in the faith, with intuitive genius, paint with such vivid
detail the landscape of shame and vulnerability. There is, for
example, the scene where the humans both try to pass the buck

for their behavior, a blaming tendency deeply enmeshed with shame. "If blame is driving," Brené Brown states simply, "shame is riding shotgun."[21] The story draws us into reflection on the very things that tend to trigger our shame defenses. The consequences God spells out for the actions of the humans revolve around childbirth, patriarchal expectations, and work—exactly the areas around which Brown's research finds men and women still continue to grapple.[22] The story exposes our fear of exile, expulsion, and abandonment; of mortality and death; of humiliation, a word that is literally derived from the word for the earth out of which, in this story, humans are created.

The story appears to end with a verdict. The humans are cast out of the garden in which they were created, in which they experienced the naked, unashamed joy and peace of unity with God. Surely, this is the ultimate cut-off, the unredeemable wrecked relationship between God, humans, and creation, destined to play out in the violence of fratricide in the story that immediately follows this one, and again and again, all down through our bloody history. Yet there is a clue, just before the humans are sent to the garden, of how God heals this wound. The humans, once naked and unashamed, now covering themselves in fear and shame, are not restored to their prior innocence, but in verse 21, God does make them new clothes. They are not sent out into the world naked. God—grieving all the while, I imagine, and weeping at the need to do so—understands the human's new reality of shame, meets them in it, and lovingly covers them.[23] Here is the vulnerable God, not thundering condemnation from above, but standing beside humanity, in our most naked, vulnerable, shivering moments, and clothing us with love.

Jan Richardson recounts how she was eventually able to discover her identity as an artist through, not accidentally, paper collage. The very act of tearing up paper, originally motivated by the conviction that none of her art was any good, became exactly the medium for her creativity, which Richardson sees as an echo of the way God works:

[P]erhaps becoming a collage artist was my way of putting those pieces back together. As I moved deeper into the artist layer of my soul, I came to experience paper collage as a spiritual practice—a form of prayer—and as a metaphor for the creative work that God does in my own life. In much the same way that I sit at my drafting table and piece together the scraps to create something new, God does this within me. God takes everything: experiences, stories, memories, relationships, dreams, prayers—all those pieces, light and dark, rough and smooth, straight and torn—and creates anew from them. I've learned to think of God as the consummate recycler: in God's economy, nothing is wasted.[24]

In God's economy, nothing—not even the terrifying experience of excruciating vulnerability, the wrecked relationship at the root of human alienation—is wasted. God recycles our experience, meets us in it, and out of our fear of nakedness makes us new clothes.

What has been seen as our paradigmatic story about sin turns out to be a story about shame and vulnerability, about broken relationship and alienation, and ultimately, we hope, about God's loving response to the nakedness, the excruciating exposure, of the human condition. In telling this story, the ancients shared insight into the human experience that continues to resonate today. They spoke about the unspeakable: the alienation, isolation, and disconnection that keeps us from experiencing unity with God, with creation, with each other, and with ourselves. Ask someone who has experienced a deep depression or suicidal ideation about alienation, isolation, and disconnection. If they are willing to talk about it, they will tell you a story about going through hell. They, like the ancient storytellers, will paint you a picture of the excruciating vulnerability of being human. The insight of Christian language is not that, in having this experience, the sufferers are somehow worse than anyone else. Rather, the language of sin reveals to us that their testimony speaks to a truth of human existence that is true for everyone, no matter how ignorant most of us are of it at any given time. Those of us who suffer from mental illness are not worse sinners, but we do have an honest, direct experience with the thing we are talking about when we talk about sin. And, I would argue, that means we also have a unique presence to offer, a unique story to share, when it comes to talking about salvation.

Traditionally, the Church's response to the reality of sin has been the practice of confession, in which the gathered believers can honestly admit their wrongdoings, repent, and receive absolution and forgiveness. Confession has been experiencing something of a revival recently. In her book *Standing Naked Before God*, United Church of Christ pastor Molly Phinney Baskette credits her congregation's practice of public confession with its turnaround from a shrinking church to a growing church. Each week, during her congregation's worship service, "a different person makes a public confession of sin and vulnerability."[25] But if sin is a fundamental experience of alienation and brokenness, what does it mean to confess? What about the person suffering from mental illness through no fault of their own—what is there for them to confess? Phinney Baskette names mental illness as one of the things members of her church might confess on a Sunday morning:

> But our sin might manifest as something that doesn't immediately sound like sin: say, clinical depression, or anxiety and control issues. . . . Of course depression, like addiction, is an illness and not a sin. But refusing treatment or keeping such issues secret from our loved ones is, because it undermines our relationship and denies God the power to help us by all possible means.[26]

I disagree somewhat with her framing. I would not call refusing treatment for mental illness a sin. I think it fails to take into account the many reasons people refuse or fail to access treatment, a topic that I'll treat in closer detail in chapter 8. It helps, however, if we remember that shame and vulnerability are center stage in our discussion of sin, a centrality which Phinney Baskette also names. Shame, remember, is different than guilt. Guilt is the sense that I have done something bad. Shame is the feeling that I am bad. We might differentiate between "small-s sins" and "capital-S Sin." Confessing sins means naming those things we have done which we ought not to have done, and that which we ought to have done yet failed to do. These things make us feel guilty. But Sin (capital S) is more than that. It's the fundamental experience of shame, and going even deeper, the core experience of disconnection and alienation.

Phinney Baskette refers to her church's practice as "a public confession of sin and vulnerability." Notice the two related but distinct terms. "Public confession of sin" sounds, to me, like a confession of wrongdoings. But public confession of vulnerability sounds like the honest sharing of hurt, shame, and stories that would otherwise be stigmatized into silence. Confession, she argues, contains both things, and it is up to the church to be the type of community where people's stigmatized, silenced, and hard-to-tell stories are voiced and heard, and where vulnerable truth-telling is welcomed with love. We are called to offer space to those who have had a close encounter with alienation and disconnection to share their testimony, for, in doing so, we are all brought closer to healing and wholeness.

What does this sort of thing look like on the psych ward? Here, I can speak only for myself. When I read the old, old story about a garden, and a snake, and two humans, I hear God's voice, echoing in the care and the love I was shown in my own time of excruciating vulnerability. I see the people who responded to me—in a time when I could feel only brokenness, and alienation, and wrecked relationship—and ultimately led me toward healing and wholeness. People who heard my wordless hurt into speech. People who asked gentle and open questions that led me to realizations about myself: Where are you right now, David? Who is telling you that you're lacking, that you're deficient? People who asked, not from a position of clinical distance, but who sat beside me, willing to risk vulnerability, to mourn with me the truth behind the questions. People who were able to meet me where I was, and work with what was there. People who, through speech, through silence, through touch, through presence, helped me put on the new clothes being offered to me by the Christ I met on the psych ward. New clothes made out of love, which, as it turns out, had a lot to do with forgiveness after all:

> "As God's chosen ones, holy and beloved, clothe yourselves with compassion, kindness, humility, meekness, and patience. Bear with one another and, if anyone has a complaint against another, forgive each other; just as the Lord has forgiven you, so you also must forgive. Above all, clothe yourselves with love, which binds everything together in perfect harmony" (Col. 3:12–14).

Notes

1. Robyn Henderson-Espinoza, "The Silent Stigma of Mental Illness in the Church," *Sojourners*, May 10, 2017, *https://sojo.net/articles/silent-stigma-mental-illness-church*.

2. Parker Palmer, *Let Your Life Speak: Listening for the Voice of Vocation* (San Francisco: John Wiley & Sons, 2000), 88.

3. Barbara Brown Taylor, *Speaking of Sin: The Lost Language of Salvation* (Boston: Cowley Publications, 2000), 5.

4. Ibid., 57–58.

5. Ibid., 62–63.

6. Susan Niditch, "Genesis," in *Women's Bible Commentary*, 3rd ed., ed. Carol A. Newsom, Sharon H. Ringe, and Jacqueline E. Lapsley (Louisville, KY: Westminster John Knox, 2012), 31.

7. Brown Taylor, *Speaking of Sin*, 47–49. The three root words Brown Taylor explores are *chatah*, *avah*, and *pasha*: "But nowhere in this [Genesis 3] story is the word "sin" mentioned, much less the phrase "original sin."

8. *The Inclusive Bible: The First Egalitarian Translation*, The Quixote Center Collective (Lanham, MD: Sheed & Ward, 2007), 6. Emphasis added.

9. Denise Dombkowski Hopkins and Michael S. Koppel, *Grounded in the Living Word: The Old Testament and Pastoral Care Practices* (Grand Rapids, MI: Eerdmans, 2010), 42.

10. Ibid., 42.

11. Brené Brown, *Daring Greatly: How the Courage to be Vulnerable Transforms the Way We Live, Love, Parent, and Lead*, (New York: Gotham, 2012), 71.

12. Ibid., 71.

13. Ibid., 68–69.

14. Ibid., 22.

15. Ibid., 76.

16. Rachel Ternes, one of the students I worked with at American University, informed me when I first presented this that the "reptilian brain" is not actually synonymous with the limbic system, which is more accurately paleomammalian; however, she has granted me absolution and the permission to continue with my metaphorical wanderings.

17. Hopkins and Koppel, *Grounded in the Living Word*, 46; with reference to Norman J. Cohen, *Hineini in Our Lives: Learning How to Respond to Others through Fourteen Biblical Texts and Personal Stories* (Woodstock, VT: Jewish Lights Publishing, 2003).

18. Interestingly enough, while up until this point the woman has been the protagonist, it is now the man who answers God. The introduction of shame into the story almost completely silences the woman, except for her later participation in the "blame game"; and the later consequences of v.16ff reinforce this patriarchal norm.

19. Brown, *Daring Greatly*, 5.

20. Jan Richardson, "In the Presence of Angels," *The Painted Prayerbook*, September 5, 2010, *http://paintedprayerbook.com/author/janrichardson/page/22/*.

21. Brown, *Daring Greatly*, 195.

22. Ibid., 86, 92ff.

23. I am indebeted to Stan Mitchell, pastor of GracePointe Church in Tennessee, for this insight. His sermon on this passage, titled "Words of Faith: Salvation," is available at *https://vimeo.com/channels/gracepointe/123277668*.

24. Richardson, "In the Presence of Angels."

25. Molly Phinney Baskette, *Standing Naked before God: The Art of Public Confession* (Cleveland: Pilgrim Press, 2015), 2.

26. Ibid., 8.

4

Sufficient

t is difficult to articulate the internal experience of mental illness.

Take depression, for example. It's easy to think of depression as an extreme form of sadness, but that's not exactly right. "Sadness" doesn't capture the paradoxical sense of being totally numb to and totally overwhelmed by emotion, simultaneously. "Very sad" as a descriptor for depression doesn't communicate the boredom, or how absolutely disgusted one gets with one's own inner voice and its unimaginative repetition of the same lies over and over and over and over. Nor does it make clear the physical pain of depression, the actual aches and soreness and fatigue. Mentally, physically, emotionally, depression is like trying to move through molasses, all while questioning the point of getting anywhere anyway. "It's like there are weights on my legs and eyebrows," I scratched into one journal in between hospitalizations. "No matter how I 'feel' I am weighed. Down. I am hurting."

Similarly, the experience of anxiety is not just that of being worried or stressed by an over-crowded to-do list. Anxiety is an overwhelming sense of paralysis. A tightening in the chest, constricting the ability to breathe. Are the walls actually closing in, or do they just seem to be? How did I end up here, on the ground, as if I were melting into the drab carpeting of this hospital ward? Like depression, anxiety is excruciatingly boring. It is so predictable in its garbage-talk that software programmer and anxiety sufferer Paul Ford was able to simulate the repetitive voice of his anxiety in a software program:

Well, anxiety, it turns out, like building this little emulator,
this anxiety simulator, made me go, oh, this part of me is
incredibly stupid. It says the same things over and over again.
And it really is like that is what my anxiety looks like. It's not
smart. At some level, it's like a little robot that just screams.
What this let me do is look at the robot.[1]

In one of my journals, I narrated a breakdown that had overwhelmed me on the psych ward:

"What happened?"
It's one of those questions I never quite have the right answer for.
"I don't know," which is true, but
maybe it was the rain
     or
this jagged feeling inside
     or
dammit, maybe I just needed a good cry
Curled up, fetal, head on couch
     Joy gets me in a chair
     Shannon talks to me, gets me medicine
the rest of the day is a fog
"What happened?"
I wanted the rain to wash me away
     to go pouring down my face
I wanted to disappear
So many things happened
     Or nothing happened
I just don't know

That's a bit of what anxiety is like—in a very controlled setting.
Take it out of the psych ward and put it in a loud Metro car or a
crowded parking lot, and perhaps you can imagine the barrier
that an everyday struggle with anxiety presents.
    Unlike depression and anxiety, mania has the advantage of
being a word we tend to reserve for conversations about mental

illness. People say they are depressed over the cancellation of a favorite show, anxious about an upcoming quiz. "Manic" doesn't dwell in our daily vocabulary in the same way. Still, it's worth clarifying: mania isn't the same as being high-energy. Mania, at least as I experience it, is aggravation, anxiety, an inability either to sit still or to focus my attention enough to go anywhere. There are physical spasms involved sometimes. Shaking. In her memoir *The Unquiet Mind*, Kay Redfield Jamison, a professor of psychiatry at Johns Hopkins School of Medicine, chronicles her lifelong experience with Type I Bipolar Disorder. She recounts a hypermanic episode, accompanied by a psychotic break with reality, characteristic of this form of the disease:

> I found myself, in that glorious illusion of high summer days, gliding, flying, now and again lurching through cloud banks and ethers, past stars, and across fields of ice crystals. Even now, I can see in my mind's rather peculiar eye an extraordinary shattering and shifting of light; inconstant but ravishing colors laid out across miles of circling rings; and the almost imperceptible, somewhat surprisingly pallid, moons of this Catherine wheel of a planet. I remember singing 'Fly Me to the Moons' as I swept past those of Saturn, and thinking myself terribly funny. I saw and experienced that which had been only dreams, or fitful fragments of aspiration. . . . The intensity, glory, and absolute assuredness of my mind's flight made it very difficult for me to believe, once I was better, that the illness was one I should willingly give up.[2]

My experience of mania, in contrast, involved no interstellar tours of Saturn. My moods simply swung wildly and randomly out of control—giddy with friends one minute, shaking and nearly crying in a cab home the next, then snarling into the mirror in my darkened basement apartment. I couldn't sleep. My mind raced. And I felt like I was moving through molasses.

When I initially checked myself into Sibley Hospital, a psychiatrist diagnosed me with a confusing web of words. "Depressive

Disorder" featured predominantly, as did many terms tagged
with the qualifier "Rule Out." As it turns out, "Rule Out"
doesn't mean "is ruled out" but instead is confusing shorthand
for "possible diagnosis." Months later, I was still navigating this
maze of terms and diagnoses when I checked myself in to yet
another acute psychiatric unit, this time at Silver Hill Hospital
in New Canaan, Connecticut. My prescribed medication didn't
seem to have much effect on my condition. One in a string of
staff psychiatrists discussed changing my medication, which led
to the following conversation:

"Have you ever been manic?" she asked.

"No." I said.

"Are you sure? It's really important, because if you've
been manic, this medication could make it worse."

"No, I'm depressed," I repeated. In my mind those were
opposites.

"Great," she intoned, and prescribed the new medication.

Two weeks later I had managed to get myself into a longer-
term care program at Silver Hill, with fewer restrictions on my
movement and activities. I had another conversation with yet
another psychiatrist. After he listened to me describe my symptoms (which I was repeating, you must understand, for approximately the gazillionth time), he put his clipboard down,
looked me in the eyes, and said, "Look, you're manic. You have
bipolar disorder."

"No," I replied. "That can't be right. I'm depressed."

"Ok," he said. "Let me get this straight." He repeated back
to me all the symptoms I had just named. "You have rapid and
extreme mood swings. You don't feel capable of regulating
your emotions—it's like they're in the driver's seat and you're
just a passenger. You feel anxious, aggravated, and unable to
sleep but at the same time constantly tired. Your thoughts are
racing and you can't keep up with them. You're able to achieve
in school, even to appear to have a mastery of difficult material,

but you feel like everything is falling apart. You find yourself obsessing over strange thoughts. You feel isolated and alone, you feel a deep shame but also have a nearly compulsive need to be around people. Is that right?"

"Yes."

"That's all hypomania. You have bipolar disorder, Type II. You should be on lithium, not on anti-depressants."

In months of seeing different psychiatrists, not a one had bothered to explain to me the difference between hypermania—the extreme highs, erratic behavior, and occasional delusions associated with Type I bipolar (as described in Jamison's book, which is what I associated with the term "manic")—and hypomania, a less extreme form of mania that can simply involve elevated or agitated moods. Even for a relatively well-informed patient such as myself, it's a complicated matter to put words and labels to complex inner experiences such as mania.

And then there's self-harm. Of all my experiences with mental illness, self-harm is the most difficult to communicate, perhaps because, at least for me, self-harm represented the end of communication, the absolute failure of speech, the falling-to-pieces of my most valuable gift: words. In between my first and second hospitalization, I wrote this in my journal after an experience of self-harm:

> I ran out of words the other night
>> and wrote non-words in cuneiform on my skin
>> cuts and lines and wedges.
>> Out of words.
> It hurts more to talk, to ask for help.
> So cut, cut, cut—
>> anger contorting and convulsing in my face
>> teeth clenched, muscles spasm-ing
> I hide blades and lighters
>> like an alcoholic hides bottles of booze

And scatter Sharpie markers everywhere
The latter, in case I have words left
    the former, in case I run out again.
    I'm sorry
    But it hurts more to speak
    when you've run out of words.

The theme of running out of words repeats over and over in my journals from that time. I was terrified by the prospect.

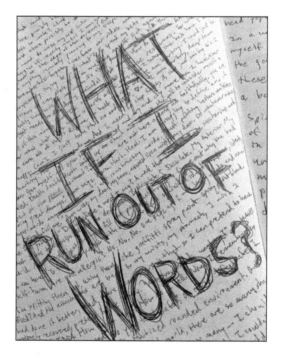

When I could find words, I used them as weapons as sharp as any blade, turning them against myself with the intent to harm, which is why I've come to understand what happened one night, in between hospitalizations, as an experience of pure grace.

I was lying in bed in my basement apartment in Northeast DC. My mother had come to stay with me for a week or so. She was on the couch upstairs, a space shared with my two housemates whose bedrooms were a floor above. I was, in other words, not really alone—my mom and two friends were within shouting distance. But, as was usual at night during those months, I felt alone. Utterly, ultimately, alone. And, as was usual, the overwhelming urge to hurt myself crashed over me like a terrifying ocean wave. Later, in therapy, I would learn an emotional regulation technique cleverly titled "Ride the Wave," which asks sufferers to imagine moments of intense emotional anguish like a wave that is powerful enough to knock you off your feet, spin you entirely around and upside down, but will also eventually wash back out to sea. It might seem eternal now, but it will, inevitably, pass. But that night I did not know that technique yet, and I got out of bed looking for something I could use to hurt myself.

Instead, I found a Sharpie marker. I don't have any particular recollection of where the idea of writing on my arm came from. I just started doing it. At the time, I don't think I saw it as a form of harm reduction, largely because what I was planning to write on myself was just as self-abusive as a physical cut would have been. I remember clearly what I intended to write on myself: "I thought you were over this."

I wanted to shame myself, to remind myself that self-harm was a problem for teenagers seeking attention—one of many stigmatizing stereotypes associated with self-harm, I now realize—not adult men on their way to a master's degree. As I started to write, something came over me: a momentary inspiration, a gracious breaking-in of . . . something. In the hospital, at a chapel service I had been allowed to attend with my parents accompanying me to ensure my safety, I heard a sermon based on 2 Corinthians 12, in which the Apostle Paul, in a fit of pique with the early church in Corinth, wrote:

But if I wish to boast, I will not be a fool, for I will be speaking the truth. But I refrain from it, so that no one may think better of me than what is seen in me or heard from me, even considering the exceptional character of the revelations. Therefore, to keep me from being too elated, a thorn was given to me in the flesh, a messenger of Satan to torment me, to keep me from being too elated. Three times I appealed to the Lord about this, that it would leave me, but he said to me, 'My grace is sufficient for you, for power is made perfect in weakness.' So, I will boast all the more gladly of my weaknesses, so that the power of Christ may dwell in me. Therefore I am content with weaknesses, insults, hardships, persecutions, and calamities for the sake of Christ; for whenever I am weak, then I am strong.

I don't remember the content of the sermon. I only know that, when the marker hit my arm, I found myself, almost against my conscious will, writing a piece of that ninth verse: "My grace is sufficient for you, for power is made perfect in weakness." I wrote that verse over and over on my arm and various other parts of my body over the following months. It was a palpable reminder of God's presence and care. It didn't always ward off self-harm, but sometimes, it did.

Sometimes. Sufficient. Enough. I have come to associate those words, in their ambiguous and underwhelming nature, with a core Christian theological concept: grace. Central to the writings of the apostle Paul and re-emphasized by the Protestant Reformers, the claim that humanity is only saved by the unmerited love and mercy of God rather than by human works is, for many, the defining mark of Christian theology. "Verily," wrote John Wesley, Anglican priest and founder of the Methodist movement, "free grace is all in all."[3] It's a powerful claim, but for me, it's the weakness of grace—its tentativeness, rather than its power—that has become its most meaningful aspect.

In his letter to the Corinthian church, Paul is apparently responding to some who have accused him of being a rather weak figure, one who was not as impressive as he is rumored to be. "I know what some people are saying," Paul writes just two chapters earlier, "his letters are severe and powerful, but in person he is weak and his speech is worth nothing" (2 Cor. 10:10, Common English Bible). It is a rather strange defense for Paul to insist not only that he is, in fact, weak, but also that God's grace is "sufficient" for him. Not abundant. Not powerful. Sufficient. Simply enough.

Paul, in fairness, is pulling a characteristic trick: claiming he isn't going to boast about himself while actually boasting about himself. "Oh, I won't boast, but I will tell you about some anonymous someone—nudge nudge, wink wink—who had these miraculous visions." Then he pauses, and takes on a truly vulnerable tone. He tells his Corinthian readers that he is hurting; really hurting. He is looking for God to take something from him, some part of him that caused him deep pain. We don't know what it is, but we know that Paul wants to be done with it. He wants an instant cure. He has to settle, instead, for grace. I love the way Paul recounts Christ's words to him, because it is such an accurate reflection of our experience with grace. "My grace is sufficient for you," God says. Sufficient. Not extravagant, necessarily. Not everything that we are looking for. Just sufficient. Enough.

Here is a simple truth about mental illness, about the diagnosis of bipolar disorder that I finally received at Silver Hill, months after my first hospitalization: there's no cure. Nobody could promise that this thing, this painful part of me that I just wanted to go away, would disappear. I prayed and prayed— trust me when I tell you, for anyone who thinks that mental illness represents a lack of faith, that I prayed and prayed and prayed—and never once did God promise to take it away from

me. I did, sometimes, get some kind of assurance. I did, sometimes, write words of faith and encouragement instead of words
of self-hate. I did feel, sometimes, the presence of God, just as
I did feel, sometimes, what seemed like the absence of God.
God had not abandoned me. I did get grace, and I had to ask
myself—and still have to ask myself every day: is this enough?

"Enough" seems like a weak word, an inadequate word
when compared to words like "abundance" and "healing," but it
carries its own power. After all, God's "power is made perfect in
weakness." Brené Brown writes of the importance of "enough"
in a culture of scarcity, characterized by the refrain "never
enough." "Given the topics I study," she says, "I know that I'm
onto something when folks look away, quickly cover their faces
with their hands, or respond with 'ouch,' 'shut up,' or 'get out
of my head.' The last is normally how people respond when
they hear or see the phrase: *Never* _____ *enough*."
She recounts how quickly the respondents in her studies are
able to fill in the blank with their own words, such as "Never
good enough," "Never perfect enough," "Never thin enough,"
"Never powerful enough," "Never successful enough," "Never
smart enough," "Never certain enough," "Never safe enough,"
and "Never extraordinary enough."[4]

In contrast to life lived from this place of scarcity, Brown
articulates a concept she calls "Wholehearted living."

> Wholehearted living is about engaging in our lives from a
> place of worthiness. It means cultivating the courage, com-
> passion, and connection to wake up in the morning and
> think, *No matter what gets done and how much is left undone, I am
> enough.* It's going to bed at night thinking, *Yes, I am imperfect
> and vulnerable and sometimes afraid, but that doesn't change the
> truth that I am also brave and worthy of love and belonging.*[5]

When I read Brown's description of the possibility of "Wholehearted living" in the midst of a culture of scarcity, I am struck
by its resonance with the way I have come to understand grace

in the midst of mental health struggles. I don't know, exactly, why my mind sometimes feels like it is out to kill me. I do know that when I experience a sense of being enough, of being sufficient, it feels like a gift from God. It feels like pure grace. It doesn't take the painful thorn from out of my side. It just restores me to some possibility of wholeness—some sort of wholeheartedness—which ultimately is the most impressive healing I could ask for. Compared to a miraculous cure or the parting of some sea, it does not seem particularly spectacular, but perhaps what we need, in a culture of scarcity, and particularly in the face of internal messages of scarcity that accompany mental health struggles, is not an extraordinary miracle, but an experience of "enough."

There is an ancient story—older even than Paul's letter to the Corinthian church—that has long served to disrupt narratives of scarcity with a message of "enough." In Exodus 16, the wandering Israelites, stranded in the desert and uncertain of their survival, awaken to find their camp covered with fine dew that, upon drying, transforms into "a fine, flaky substance." Baffled, the Israelites ask, "What is it?"—in Hebrew, *man hu,* which becomes the name for the mysterious substance: manna. The Israelites are given explicit instructions for gathering the heavenly what-is-it: gather only as much as they need and no more. Gather only enough. Remarkably, those who disobey and gather more than their family needs find the surplus disappears. Those who try to save some for tomorrow find it has spoiled. There is no way to hoard manna, whatever it might be. One can have only enough of it—never more, and never less.

The story of manna in the wilderness, as part of the paradigmatic Exodus narrative, has clear economic implications for later generations.[6] In fact, Paul refers to the story in his letter to the Corinthians to emphasize the need for equity and balance between abundance and need (2 Cor. 8:13–15). If the message of Exodus was directed toward the tendency of an ancient society to divide itself between the hoarding of wealth and the deprivations of poverty, then certainly an economics of "enough" is as relevant and subversive as ever. As I re-read the story, however, I am struck on a more personal level. In the wilderness wanderings of mental health struggle, the supposed abundance of a distant promised land seems like an unrealistic fantasy. Mental illness has a compounding effect. It is not only the suffering itself that is difficult to bear, but also the seemingly certain promise of future suffering. An inner voice seems to whisper, "You will never feel better." To this, the counter-argument—"Of course you will feel better!"— seems hollow at best, and, at worst, cruel.

The divine promise of manna, of gracious bread from heaven, is different. It is God's reminder to look for the "enough," gathering like dew on the surface of the very ground from which it is difficult for the sufferers to lift their eyes. Such provision cannot be hoarded. It will often feel scarce. It is a miracle in a minor key: a Sharpie instead of a blade; a friend's visit or letter instead of isolation; a day or an hour or a minute without a breakdown. "My grace," God told Paul, and the Israelites in the desert, "is sufficient for you." It doesn't seem like much, but it might just be enough.

In the hospital, I developed the habit of verbally assigning small happenings to what I called "the victory column." Got out of bed in the morning? One for the victory column. Finished a meal? Took a shower? Victory column. Occasionally, one or two of my ward-mates would pick up on the practice. It was a way of naming aloud the small wins that, in normal times, might not even be noticed, but seemed to us like the overcoming of insurmountable obstacles. Although I didn't think of it at the time, it was my way of collecting manna—not enough to hoard, just enough to make it through the next moment, and then the next. The accomplishments in the victory column might seem negligible, perhaps even pathetic, to someone in better health. Perhaps not. Perhaps we are all in need of a victory column. Perhaps we are all struggling, longing for an abundance that seems always out of reach, missing the manna collecting at our feet.

The word "enough" has another sense, another layer of meaning, that speaks directly into my experience of mental illness. Psalm 46 tells of God's presence and protection in the midst of great turmoil. Its tenth verse is often quoted on mugs and bookmarks and desk calendars: "Be still, and know that I am God." It is, or at least it seems to be, a counsel of calm and quiet in the midst of life's storms.

The recent Common English Bible (CEB) translation of the psalm, however, renders the verse differently: "That's enough! Now know that I am God!" The CEB translators are onto something. Robert Alter translates the verse, "Let go, and know that I am God," commenting, "The verb—etymologically, it means to relax one's grip on something—is somewhat surprising here. It might be an injunction to cease and desist from armed struggle, to unclench the warrior's fist," an interpretation that makes sense given the preceding verses refer to God ending war and destroying weaponry.[7] Yet another translation reads, "An end to your fighting!"[8] The connotation of "enough" is a bit different than that of "be still." God sounds exasperated. "That's enough! Stop that!"

Jesus uses a similarly ambiguous term in one of his last conversations with his followers before his death. In Luke's gospel, just before Jesus' arrest, as he tries one final time to warn the disciples of the coming events, the following exchange occurs:

> He said to them, 'When I sent you out without a purse, bag, or sandals, did you lack anything?' They said, 'No, not a thing.' He said to them, 'But now, the one who has a purse must take it, and likewise a bag. And the one who

has no sword must sell his cloak and buy one. For I tell you, this scripture must be fulfilled in me, 'And he was counted among the lawless'; and indeed, what is written about me is being fulfilled.' They said, 'Lord, look, here are two swords.' He replied, 'It is enough.' (Luke 22:25–38)

Translated in this fashion, Jesus seems to be advising his disciples in how to prepare themselves materially for the coming struggle. But his final sentence is rendered with a small but important difference by the Common English Bible: "He replied, 'Enough of that!'" The verb, in Greek, is *hikanos*, and can be translated as "enough" or "sufficient." Perhaps the disciples missed the irony of Jesus' words. Taking nothing with them for their journey, they had lacked nothing, always having what they needed—always having enough. Now, as Jesus tries to explain how difficult the coming trials will be, and how differently the disciples are to act when compared to the power-focused ways of the world (Luke 22:24–27), the disciples reveal that they've been holding back, hiding weapons on their persons rather than trusting in divine provisions. It's not that two swords are enough swords to get them through the coming days, it's that Jesus has had enough of his followers' arguments, grumblings, and misunderstandings. "That's enough!" "Cease your fighting!" "Let go of your weapons!"

In another account, Jesus's final words on the cross are, "It is finished" (John 19:28). The word in Greek is the same word translated as "perfect" in the passage from Paul which I wrote on my wrist: "My grace is sufficient for you, for power is made perfect in weakness." I can imagine Jesus, hanging his head on the Cross, whispering to himself, "It's finished. Stop this. That's enough."

"That's enough." This, too, is a message of grace. As the Sharpie marker hovered over my skin, poised to express my self-loathing and shame, it was as if a gentle hand took hold of mine and said, "That's enough. Cease your fighting. Be still." And some love beyond my ability wrote out on my skin,

"My grace is sufficient for you." For power, you see, is finished, in weakness.

Why was I able to experience this grace, to pick up the marker instead of the blade, while others are not? Why do some people who experience suicidal ideation survive, while others do not? I have no idea. I know it's not because of any particular virtue on my part, nor any particular vice on the part of those who die by suicide. Some survive, and some do not, and I don't know why. Parker Palmer recounts a time when he was asked this question by a woman who was struggling with her own depression, and he describes his inability to come up with a satisfactory answer. After their conversation, he ruminated, wondering if he could have found something more helpful to say. His conversation partner ended up writing him to thank him for his honest confession of unknowing. "My response," he writes, "had given her an alternative to the cruel 'Christian explanations' common in the church to which she belonged— that people who take their lives lack faith or good works or some other redeeming virtue that might move God to rescue them. My not knowing had freed her to stop judging herself for being depressed and to stop believing that God was judging her."[9] Sometimes, our unknowing is all we have to offer. Sometimes, it's our silent presence. Sometimes, we realize we have been unable to help, and we hope against hope that someone who suffered so much has experienced, in some way beyond our understanding, some sort of peace or comfort they were unable to find in life. We hold them in our love and our care and we pray that somehow, that is enough.

The church has a practice that acknowledges the sufficiency, the enough-ness, of grace. It is an ancient practice, and yet in its multi-sensory, participatory, and deeply symbolic nature, oddly suited for a post-modern world. It has gone by many names, among them the Lord's Supper, Holy Communion, and the Eucharist. The last comes from a Greek word for "thanksgiving," in turn rooted in a word for "gift" or "grace." In the Methodist tradition in which I was raised and formed, communion is one of the "means of grace"—not something we do to earn grace, but rather a practice that "puts us in the way" of grace. John Wesley, one of Methodism's founders, referred to it as an "ordinary means of grace," and it is, indeed, quite ordinary. The meal shared in communion is simple, even meager. It consists of bread, broken and crumbling, and wine—or, for Methodists and Baptists, perhaps just pasteurized grape juice. Those partaking in the meal might gather around a small table, or come forward one by one to receive a gift that is, by most measures, quite mundane. As we take the bread and the fruit of the vine, we participate in the solidarity of God as experienced in Christ on the Cross. We let go of our weapons, we disarm and un-armor ourselves to participate in this ceremony of vulnerability. How much more fragile could a ritual be than the communal sharing of crumbling bread and simple juice? As we rip apart the bread, crumbs scatter and drop to the ground. It is an experience of both brokenness and wholeness. Just as the story of wandering nomads collecting scraps of bread they hope will be enough is paradigmatic for the biblical narrative, so, too, this unimpressive meal, this sharing of something that doesn't look like much of a feast, is paradigmatic for the activity of the church. As Christians, we gather for worship and for community, and it is not the ringing of heavenly voices. We do small acts for justice, we serve in our communities, we go to rallies or write to our members of Congress, and it is not the reign of God come on earth. It is just a few of us up against systems of oppression and injustice and violence that seem to go on and on. We are anointed with oil and all of our aches and pains and problems do not magically disappear. And yet, we keep doing these things. We keep pointing toward our hope in a kingdom yet to come. We keep discovering God and each other, God in each other. We keep believing that these small acts, like grace, can be transformative, can move us to somewhere we have not yet been. It may not seem like much. It may not always seem like a miracle. But it might just be enough.

Notes

1. "If You Don't Have Anything Nice to Say, SAY IT IN ALL CAPS," January 23, 2015, episode 545, *This American Life, http://www.thisamericanlife.org/radio-archives/episode/545 /transcript.*

2. Kay Redfield Jamison, *An Unquiet Mind: A Memoir of Moods and Madness* (New York: Vintage Books, 1996), 90–91.

3. John Wesley, "Free Grace," Sermon 110 (1739), in *John Wesley's Sermons: An Anthology,* ed. Albert C. Outler and Richard P. Hetizenrater (Nashville, TN: Abingdon, 1991), 50.

4. Brené Brown, *Daring Greatly: How the Courage to be Vulnerable Transforms the Way We Live, Love, Parent, and Lead* (New York: Gotham, 2012), 24–25.

5. Ibid., 10. Emphasis in original.

6. Bruce C. Birch, Walter Brueggemann, Terence E. Fretheim, and David L. Petersen, *A Theological Introduction to the Old Testament,* 2nd ed. (Nashville, TN: Abingdon, 2005), 124.

7. Robert Alter, *The Book of Psalms: A Translation with Commentary* (New York: W. W. Norton & Co., 2007), 165.

8. *The Psalter: A Faithful and Inclusive Rendering from the Hebrew into Contemporary English,* ed. International Commission on English in the Liturgy (Chicago: Liturgy Training Publications, 1995).

9. Parker Palmer, *Let Your Life Speak: Listening for the Voice of Vocation* (San Francisco: John Wiley & Sons, 2000), 59.

5

God's Sleeves

On July 3, 2011, I wrote in my journal after a morning incident in the Sibley Hospital psych ward. I don't have a strong memory of what was going on in my head at the time. All I know is that I left the breakfast table after sneaking a plastic knife into my pocket. I then went into the bathroom, sat down on the floor, and starting trying to cut my wrists open. I don't blame you if you're thinking, "What did you possibly think you could do with a plastic utensil?" Clearly, I was not in a particularly rational frame of mind. Self-harm has many characteristics of compulsive or addictive behavior; while I don't remember specifics, it's clear my mind was turning in on itself particularly fiercely that day. It was the first time I tried to hurt myself while in the hospital.

The bathrooms on psych wards don't lock, for exactly this sort of reason. It didn't take long for a nurse to notice I was missing, knock, then push into the bathroom and grab the plastic knife from me. Later that day, after I had calmed down—and after the dose of anti-anxiety medication had kicked in—I wrote in my journal:

> Things that a nurse says to you after you realize you want to cut your wrist with a plastic butter knife:
>
> "You might think of this as your body and mind sending you a message, saying—don't forget, you still have a lot of healing to do."
>
> (and I think of the thorn in Paul's side to keep him from being too elated)

Or

"This is a process, but it is like an upward spiral. You can't think of this as going backwards, but as a painful part of the process toward healing."

Or

"You have a theological background, so think of the wind that blows where it will. The same wind that brought you to this hurtful place is the wind of healing that is going to blow you to places of happiness and wholeness. It is one wind, and we don't always know where it takes us, but we are trusting it is all part of the process of healing."

And

"I am just trying to give you some images to help you grasp this. If they are helpful, fine, if not, fine too."

In the end I take an Ativan, but still, the talking helps. Another angel.

The entry is followed by a poorly scribbled illustration:

The text below the drawing reads: "Christ on the psych ward. If you don't think God can be a woman, you've never needed a nurse."

✝

First, let me state the (hopefully) obvious: not all nurses are women, just as not all doctors are men. The nurses on Sibley's psych ward during my stays there were women, although that was not the case at Silver Hill Hospital, where many of the nurses were men. Several of the rotating cast of psychiatrists who diagnosed me were women; several others were men. I state what might seem obvious to some because, until quite recently, it would not have been obvious at all. Societal assumptions about gender (among a host of other identities) and their attendant workplace expectations continue to hold power. How we imagine various roles, and who we imagine occupying them, has real effects not only in terms of access but in terms of fair pay and treatment in the workplace.

If it matters who we can imagine holding certain positions and roles, then it also matters how we imagine God. In the words of Howard Thurman, "the object of one's belief has to do with that which is central to one's life."[1] How we imagine God—the images and metaphors and descriptors that we associate with the centrality of our life—affects how we understand the world and our priorities within it, and vice versa. If our images of God are limited, our understanding of God's activity in our lives and our response to that activity will be similarly limited. South African pastor and theologian Trevor Hudson puts it this way:

> Over the years I have become convinced of the importance of how we understand God. Who is the God we worship? What is our God like? These questions are important because we become like the God we worship. . . . Our picture of God has a way of rubbing off on us, shaping the way we see the world, the way we relate to those who suffer, the way we respond to our enemies.[2]

When we picture God, whom or what do we picture? All of us—even those of us who did not grow up within a particular religious tradition—have some sort of image of God that we absorbed, largely subconsciously, while growing up. Theologians refer to this as an "embedded theology," one which has developed throughout our lifetime without our paying any particular attention to it. Often these embedded God images include God as Father, Shepherd, or Almighty King. These images are predominantly male, and emphasize power and majesty, as theologian Elizabeth Johnson points out:

> The precise idea from the world of men that has provided the paradigm for the symbol of God is the ruling man within a patriarchal system. Divine mystery is cast in the role of a monarch, absolute ruler, King of Kings, Lord of Lords, one whose will none can escape, to whom is owed total and unquestioning obedience. This powerful monarch is sometimes spoken of as just and harsh, threatening hell fire to sinners who do not measure up. But even when he is presented as kindly, merciful, and forgiving, the fundamental problem remains. Benevolent patriarchy is still patriarchy.[3]

If God is always imagined as a patriarch, our understanding of God is limited. If God is always pictured as a male, our picture of God, and of the world, is incomplete.

How I see God matters to me, not only in theory, but in a very concrete and, one might say, incarnate way because my need for God does not exist in some distant time or plane of existence, but in places like the one depicted by my inexpertly drawn image: curled up by the nurses' station, with a woman who was kind and also firm, caring and also strong, lifting me up out of the pit I had been folded into by pain and mental anguish. Later, she sat with me and shared needed wisdom (Wisdom being just one of many female images of God in the scriptures), speaking of the divine wind and saying, "I am just trying to give you some images to help you grasp this." Little wonder I labeled my picture "Christ on the Psych Ward." Who in this story was performing the activities associated with Christ? Who was saving? Healing? Teaching? Accompanying? Comforting? Of course, the nurse who pulled me off the floor of the psych ward that day was not Jesus. She would laugh off such a suggestion, I'm sure. And my experience of being helped, saved, comforted, healed, taught by her changed how I imagined God, which should not be a surprise, for our language about God, including biblical language about God, is mediated in and through human imagery and our limited material reality.

"My God, my God, why have you forsaken me?" pleads the famous opening line of Psalm 22. Less well known, perhaps, are verses 9–10: "Yet it was you who took me from the womb; you kept me safe on my mother's breast. On you I was cast from my birth, and since my mother bore me you have been my God." These are powerful images of God's care and one of many biblical passages in which God is conceived of as female. Who, in ancient Israel, would be responsible for taking a baby from the womb and placing the newborn safely on the mother's breast? Not a man. God is a midwife, performing a role that would have been both sacred and taboo, but definitely women's work in Hebrew culture. "Do not be far from me," the psalmist continues, "for trouble is near and there is no one to help." The psalmist begs the midwife-God to remain close for both comfort and protection.

The last word—protection—is important. It's entirely possible to use feminine imagery for God that simply reinforces the stereotypical division of men's work and women's work. Delving into a multiplicity of divine images allows the various layers and implications of these images to challenge and complicate each other. The midwife-God is nurturing and also protective in times of danger. You don't want to mess with the image of

God in Hosea 13:8: "I will fall upon them like a bear robbed of her cubs, and will tear open the covering of their heart." Mama bear is not exactly sweet and patient. Images of God are remarkably fluid, able to flow in and out of each other so that God peeks out from behind descriptions of both midwife and mother, father and feathered bird.

This fluidity is important because our tendency to think of God as male is not our only kind of limiting imagery. It wouldn't take a newcomer to Christianity a very long time to notice that Christians love to talk about light. Scripture describes Jesus as "the light of the world" (John 8:12) and tells us that "in him there is no darkness at all" (1 John 1:5). The Christian community is supposed to be a light to the world as well (Matthew 5:14). The images pile up after a while, leading to an obvious conclusion: light is good, and dark is bad.

The metaphor makes sense in a lot of ways. There is something about our faith that tends us toward language about illumination, about being able to see or to understand in a new way. There is something powerful, too, something visceral, about the connection between darkness and uncertainty or struggle. There are also some unintended consequences to the ease of our metaphorical preference for light. In her book *Learning to Walk in the Dark*, Barbara Brown Taylor writes:

> At the theological level, however, this language creates all sorts of problems. It divides every day in two, pitting the light part against the dark part. It tucks all the sinister stuff into the dark part, identifying God with the sunny part and leaving you to deal with the rest on your own time. It implies things about dark-skinned people and sight-impaired people that are not true. Worst of all, it offers people of faith a giant closet in which they can store everything that threatens or frightens them without thinking too much about those things. . . . To embrace that teaching and others like it at face value can result in a kind of spirituality that deals with

darkness by denying its existence or at least depriving it of
any meaningful attention. I call it "full solar spirituality."[4]

The United States, among other nations, has seen the
obvious horrifying consequences of a "light good, dark bad"
division throughout our history. As the Black Lives Matters
movement has reminded us, the injustices created by this division are not a thing of the past. Of course, there is more to
our ongoing struggles with racial prejudice in this country
than metaphors about light and dark, but it doesn't help with
the unconscious biases of our society that we so often associate darkness with evil or pain. Jesus himself had to deal with
his disciples making assumptions about a man with impaired
vision when they asked, "Rabbi, who sinned, this man or his
parents, that he was born blind?" (John 9:2) Our preference
for light and sight can lead to some problematic stuff.

Barbara Brown Taylor emphasizes the extent to which
such thinking leaves us incapable of facing times of doubt or
struggle:

> You can usually recognize a full solar church by its emphasis
> on the *benefits* of faith, which include a sure sense of God's
> presence, certainty of belief, divine guidance in all things,
> and reliable answers to prayer. Members strive to be positive
> in attitude, firm in conviction, helpful in relationship, and
> unwavering in faith.[5]

She adds,

> There are days when I would give anything to share their
> vision of the world and their ability to navigate it safely, but
> my spiritual gifts do not seem to include the gift of solar spir-
> ituality. Instead, I have been given the gift of lunar spiritual-
> ity, in which the divine light available to me waxes and wanes
> with the season. . . . All in all, the moon is a truer mirror
> for my soul than the sun that looks the same way every day.[6]

Isaiah 45:3 recounts God saying: "I will give you the treasures of darkness, and riches hidden in secret places, so that
you may know that it is I, the LORD, who call you by your
name." I have often thought of my struggles with mental illness
in terms of darkness, but this passage rings true for me: the
darkness has its treasures and its hidden riches. A pastor friend
who came to visit me in the hospital brought me a translation
of Rainer Maria Rilke's *Book of Hours.* My journals from the hospital are filled with quotations from the book, many of which
evoke divine darkness:

> But when I lean over the chasm of myself—
> it seems
> my God is dark
> and like a web: a hundred roots
> silently drinking.[7]

or

> You, darkness, of whom I am born—
> I love you more than the flame
> that limits the world
> to the circle it illumines
> and excludes all the rest.
> But the darkness embraces everything;
> shapes and shadows, creatures and me,
> people, nations—just as they are.
> It lets me imagine
> a great presence stirring beside me.
> I believe in the night.[8]

To be able to imagine God in the darkness—and to value
the darkness as mysterious, as grounding, as nourishing, as
all-inclusive—is a powerful anecdote to what Brown Taylor
terms "full solar spirituality." Mental illness, for me, has been
an experience of darkness in many ways. Yet darkness can
also be healing, even as light can be jarring. In contrast to the

bright lights of the psych ward, or the night duty nurse shining a flashlight into the room every ten minutes for a safety check, often interrupting sleep, darkness can feel like a comfort. God, after all, created both light and dark. (Isaiah 45:7) God is present, is close, in both.

When I read Psalm 22, I read the despairing song of a person who feels abandoned, isolated, alienated; one who cries out for God, more than anything else, to stay close, to be with him or her. "But I am a worm, and not human," sobs the psalmist, in language that is hyperbolic, even pathetic, and, in the midst of a breakdown, exactly what I felt. The psalmist is "scorned by others, and despised by the people." It is an isolated, lonely, hurting person who cries out for the midwife-God, begging for help in the midst of danger, real or imagined: "Many bulls encircle me, strong bulls of Bashan surround me; they open wide their mouths at me, like a ravening and roaring lion" (v.12–13). The midwife-God is also a strong defender of Her charge. Therefore, God's deliverance can be proclaimed "to a people yet unborn," because God is in the business both of creating and of protecting.

While I might not have been able to put language to this at the time, the layers of meaning within the psalmist's images of God had a liberating importance to me in the midst of mental and emotional turmoil. A mighty yet distant king was of no use to me on the psych ward. I already felt disconnected and distant, and it was the nearby nurses, doctors, and social workers who were doing the work to calm the raging storm in my brain. In fact, the more "powerful" of those figures—the psychiatrists—were the ones with whom I had the least interaction and, correspondingly, the ones about whom I felt the most ambivalent. The nurses and social workers, on the other hand, were the more reliable companions on my rocky journey.[9] The image of God as a distant king, or even a rarely available doctor, only worked to exacerbate my suffering. But God as a companion, healer, or caretaker? All of these images, in both biblical and modern-day forms, were able to get in underneath my pain and shore up my fragile sense that I was not alone and that I might even be able to survive after all.

One of the images of God that accompanied me during my time on the psych ward came to me prior to my hospitalization, in the midst of what I can now identify as the beginning of a manic episode. I was with friends, playing guitar, and half-jokingly started writing a song that, somewhat to my surprise, then wrote itself. Looking back, I can see how I was careening toward a mental and emotional cliff. The words and images that flowed so quickly during that time were wonderful, but they were also evidence of my brain's erratic activity. I wrote many songs, poems, and prose pieces during that time, but I was also falling apart internally. Many people who could successfully receive treatment for bipolar disorder refuse to do so because they don't want to lose out on the creativity of the manic periods. I can understand. There is something intoxicating about the racing thoughts and odd obsessions that characterize mania, even of the lesser, hypomanic kind. Of course, like being overly intoxicated, the fun ends, often catastrophically. Yet the question of how to treat bipolar disorder without undermining the creativity and personality of those suffering remains a real one.

Drawing on imagery from the final chapters of the book of Revelation, the song I wrote has become one of my favorite pieces. Its first lines arrived like this: "If the leaves of the tree are for the healing of the nations, then/we're gonna need a lot of leaves./And if God's gonna wipe every tear from every eye, then/She's gonna need some real big sleeves." In one of many mystical visions of the healing of creation contained in this bizarre but visually rich apocalyptic text, Revelation 7:17

describes God as a Lamb who will wipe away tears: "The Lamb at the center of the throne will be their shepherd, and he will guide them to springs of the water of life, and God will wipe away every tear from their eyes." The text uses masculine pronouns, and yet when I first sang the lyrics to what would become "God's Sleeves," it seemed obvious to me that the God wiping tears from all our eyes would be a woman. It was hard for me to imagine a man wiping tears from my eyes. I was willing to play with the gender of God in the song, but it is harder for me to play with ideas of gender in my human interactions, which says much more about me and about our cultural hang-ups around gender than it does about God.

Soon after the incident with the plastic knife, my parents came to visit me in the hospital. My dad, who also struggles with mental illness, sat next to me and told me, "You will keep going. You will feel better. Even if it's shitty." And then he started crying. After they left I wrote about the visit in my journal: "I saw my dad cry, yesterday. I don't know where to put that."

Years earlier, my dad had talked to me about his own mental health struggles, a conversation that had not come easily for him. Mental illness had likely run in our family for generations, but had also remained a family secret, never spoken about openly or honestly. My parents both made a concerted effort to break the silence about mental illness in the family, which is something that men in the U.S. are simply not socialized to do. It involves admitting weakness and vulnerability. Herbert Anderson, a professor of pastoral theology, writes that many men have been raised to believe that "the mark of being a man is to suffer in silence: showing pain is a sign of vulnerability or weakness." As a result, "the pain of sadness is compounded by loneliness and isolation."[10] Maintaining the illusion of strength and dominance is itself an unhealthy effort. A recent study in the *Journal of Counseling Psychology* reveals that conforming to the standards of traditional masculinity leads to mental health problems.[11] My dad's earlier vulnerability in discussing his mental health struggles was, I see now, an act of great courage. And yet the sight of my dad crying was confusing and disorienting. I was witnessing something taboo: an alternative image of what it meant to be a man.

Images matter. How we imagine the divine and the relationship between the divine and humanity affects how we imagine our human relationships as well. God as Father is certainly a staple of Christian imagery. When we imagine God as Father, what kind of father do we imagine? I had never imagined a father with shoulders shaking, hand covering his face, weeping over the suffering of his son, feeling, perhaps, some level of responsibility for the slumped-over, shrunken-down figure in front of him. "Cultural bias against men who weep spills over into our God images," writes Denise Dombkowski Hopkins, a scholar of the Hebrew Bible. "Too often in many societies . . . tears are seen as a sign of weakness and are associated with women."[12]

Can God cry? The scriptures certainly think so. Dombkowski Hopkins observes that the image of the weeping God in the book of Jeremiah is often concealed by translators:

> God also weeps. Some are reluctant to attribute grief to God because their core testimony affirms a God of strength. Tears signal divine weakness and vulnerability. . . . Disagreements over the translation of Jeremiah 9:10 express this reluctance. The NRSV, following some versions, translates the verse as God's command to the people: 'Take up weeping and wailing for the mountains. . . .' The NIV, following the Hebrew text, translates with God as the subject: 'I will take up weeping and wailing. . . .' God is both mourner and mourned for. . . . God grieves *with* the people over their destruction. God grieves *because* the people have broken their covenant relationship with God.[13]

This is more than some obscure translation debate. It concerns not only the nature of God but also the nature of humanity's relationship to the divine. "The psalmist's tears," Dombkowski Hopkins writes, "function positively as a prompt for God's hoped-for empathetic response," reflecting the way that tears "express our need for connection."[14] Tears are both a way to mourn and a way to reach out, to show the sort of vulnerability that invites empathy, connection, and, ultimately, relationship. My dad was crying on the psych ward, mourning his son's hurt and also, perhaps, instinctively trying to establish an empathetic connection. That I was unsure how to respond was perhaps indicative of my own sense of disconnection, not only from my father but also from my own body, my own emotions, my own self. As my dad was crying, perhaps God was crying, too. Crying in empathy, in connection, in solidarity with his psych-ward-bound child.

Trevor Hudson, reflecting on Romans 8:22–27, identifies three groans—the groans of creation, the groans of the Spirit, and our own human groaning—that are simultaneously crying out together for healing and redemption. "Believing that God groans with us," he writes, "challenges our picture of God."[15] What's more, we are able to find the groaning God, the crying God, by being attentive to our own groaning and tears. Hudson recounts a time when he asked Gordon Crosby, founder of the Church of the Savior in Washington, DC, for advice. Crosby responded: "When you go back to South Africa and stand up to preach and teach, remember always that each person sits next to their own pool of tears."[16]

Each of us sits next to our own pool of tears. That's a whole lot of tears. If God is going to wipe every tear from every eye, then she is indeed going to need some really big sleeves. What's more, the God who will wipe every tear from every eye is a God who cries. The divine wiping away of tears is the looked-for empathetic response of weeping humans, and comes only after God responds with tears of her own. God does not wipe away our tears out of discomfort. God was much more comfortable with my dad's shuddering shoulders than I was. God was and is reaching out, trying to connect, trying to cross the chasm. Reimagining God, I hope, opens up a conversation about reimagining humanity. Perhaps it even allows us to move past our tendency toward binary ways of thinking: male/female, dark/light, divine/human. Each pair of images is separated by a chasm much deeper than a simple slash mark can truly indicate. When we reimagine the chasm as a continuum, we move into images that are more expansive and more inclusive of relationship and connection.

"If you don't think God can be a woman," I wrote, "you've never needed a nurse." I could have written, "If you don't think God can be person, you've never needed a nurse." I needed the Christ I met on the psych ward to be embodied because my mental illness undermined my own sense of integration and embodiment. When we trace the scriptural narrative of embodiment, of incarnation, we go on the very journey I have taken with this chapter: from a diversity of images of God, to a transcending of human categories of God, to the transcending even of the division between divine and human. Earlier, I briefly mentioned Wisdom as one of the Bible's many feminine images of God. Wisdom (Hebrew *hokhmah*, Greek *sophia*) is featured prominently in the book of Proverbs, where she is personified as a woman who teaches the people and leads them in God's ways, and who partners with God in the work of creation (Proverbs 8). In the introduction to the *Wisdom Commentary* series, Barbara Reid summarizes the importance of the figure she refers to as "Woman Wisdom":

> In the Scriptures, Woman Wisdom appears as 'a breath of the power of God, and a pure emanation of the glory of the Almighty' (Wis 7:25), who was present and active in fashioning all that exists (Prov 8:22–31; Wis 8:6). She is a spirit who pervades and penetrates all things (Wis 7:22–23), and she provides guidance and nourishment at her all-inclusive table (Prov 9:1–5).[17]

The Hebrew Bible imagery of Woman Wisdom is reflected, in many ways, in New Testament language about Jesus. It is no accident that the description of Wisdom as "a pure emanation of the glory of the Almighty" bears striking resemblance to the description of Christ as "the reflection of God's glory" in the Epistle to the Hebrews—the very verse that evoked for me the image of Christ on the psych ward. Reid points out a number of passages in which scripture "portrays Jesus as Wisdom incarnate."[18] One of these portrayals has become particularly important for feminist readings of the New Testament: the "numerous parallels between what is said of Wisdom and of the *Logos* in the Prologue of the Fourth Gospel (John 1:1–18).[19]

Logos is the biblical Greek word usually translated as "Word" in the opening lines of the Gospel of John: "In the beginning was the Word, and the Word was with God, and the Word was God." All things were created through this *Logos*, according to John 1:3, in language strikingly similar to Proverbs 8:22–31. "Jesus is Sophia incarnate, the Wisdom of God," [20] writes Elizabeth Johnson, "Wisdom Made Flesh."[21] She goes on:

> Not only does the gender symbolism cast Jesus into an inclusive framework with regard to his relationships with human beings and with God, removing the male emphasis that so quickly turns to androcentrism. But, the symbol giving rise to thought, it also evokes Sophia's characteristic gracious goodness, life-giving creativity, and passion for justice as key hermeneutical elements in speaking about the mission of Jesus.[22]

From a way of imagining God as a woman to a way of understanding Jesus as transgressing the boundaries of gender—in Christ, Paul writes, "there is no longer male or female" (Gal 3:28)—we arrive at the Incarnate Christ who crosses the divide between divine and human, taking on flesh to live among us. That is the Christ I encountered on the psych ward, taking on flesh in the strong hands and the kind yet honest words of a nurse; embodied in the care of friends and fellow patients;

revealed in the tears of my father. We find this Christ sharing divine vulnerability and weakness by weeping with others at the grave of a friend, the Resurrection and the Life still mourning the pain of death (John 11:25–35), the Divine and Human One crying tears of empathy and connection. And it is this very Jesus, this Wisdom made Flesh, this One who is Human and Divine, feminine and masculine, darkness and light, who turns to the disciples in a dimly lit room and names them with a simple word: "friends."

Notes

1. Howard Thurman, *Deep Is the Hunger: Meditations for Apostles of Sensitiveness* (Richmond, IN: Friends United Press, 1978), 152.

2. Trevor Hudson with Stephen Bryant, *Listening to the Groans: A Spirituality for Ministry and Mission* (Nashville, TN: Upper Room Books, 2007), 33–34.

3. Elizabeth Johnson, *She Who Is: The Mystery of God in Feminist Theological Discourse* (1992; New York: Crossroad, 2002), 34.

4. Barbara Brown Taylor, *Learning to Walk in the Dark* (San Francisco: HarperOne, 2014), 7

5. Ibid., 7.

6. Ibid., 8–9.

7. Rainer Maria Rilke, *Rilke's Book of Hours*, trans. Anita Barrows and Joanna Macy (New York: Riverhead Books, 2005), 47.

8. Ibid., 63.

9. I don't mean to impugn the psychiatrists I have worked with over the years. As I discuss in a later chapter, they are themselves limited by a system that is simply not designed well to meet the needs of those with mental health struggles.

10. Herbert Anderson, "Men and Grief: The Hidden Sea of Tears without Outlet," in *The Care of Men*, ed. Christie Cozad Neuger and James Newton Poling (Nashville, TN: Abingdon, 1997), 205.

11. "Sexism May Be Harmful to Men's Mental Health," *American Psychological Association*, November 22, 2016, *http://www.apa.org/news/press/releases/2016/11/sexism-harmful .aspx*.

12. Denise Dombkowski Hopkins, *Psalms Books 2–3*, in *Wisdom Commentary* series, vol. 21, ed. Barbara E. Reid, O.P. (Collegeville, MN: Liturgical Press, 2016), 9.

13. Denise Dombkowski Hopkins and Michael S. Koppel, *Grounded in the Living Word: The Old Testament and Pastoral Care Practices* (Grand Rapids, MI: William B. Eerdmans, 2010), 147.

14. Dombkowski Hopkins, *Psalms Books 2–3*, 8–9.

15. Hudson and Bryant, *Listening to the Groans*, 33.

16. Ibid., 28.

17. Barbara E. Reid, O.P., "Editor's Introduction to Wisdom Commentary: 'She Is a Breath of the Power of God' (Wis 7:25)," in *Wisdom Commentary*, vol. 21 (Collegeville, MN: Liturgical Press, 2016), xxiii.

18. Ibid.

19. Ibid.

20. Johnson, *She Who Is*, 156.

21. Ibid., 150.

22. Ibid., 157.

6

God's Friends

n the hospital, there were social workers who led group activities on topics relevant to our struggles. One day, they led an exercise on support systems. They asked us to make a list of five supports in our lives, five people or things that we could rely on in times of need. At the time, I was almost incapable of thinking of positive things in my life. Everything seemed awful and everything hurt. But five supports? In a detached, factual sort of way, I thought I could do that. The chaplain who drove me to the hospital and then stayed with me for eight hours while I checked in; the pastor of my own church in DC who came and visited regularly; friends from seminary who visited nearly every day; my parents who had driven up the east coast from North Carolina to visit me; a pastor friend who came to visit, served me communion, and then shared the extra bread with another patient who spread butter on the Body of Christ. Internally, I felt alone, isolated, and abandoned, but when asked to list names, I could do it easily. I was the only person in the group who could name five supports. One person could not name one. I remember being shocked. I was feeling incredibly isolated, painfully alone. But if I, with my legion of support, was feeling alone, what did I have to say to my fellow patients? Did I have anything to offer to people who experienced such loneliness?

Loneliness is a ghost. It haunts the halls of psych wards and prisons, of high powered firms and of prestigious universities. Loneliness is one sign, one symptom, of the brokenness of the world in which we live and move and serve. By loneliness, I don't just mean being alone. We all need alone time. Solitude is a powerful spiritual practice. But that ache. That hurt. That desperate longing for someone to share intimate time and space with us. That is something beyond just being alone.

Our scriptures witness to the power of loneliness. "You have caused friend and neighbor to shun me," howls the author of Psalm 88, "my companions are in darkness." These words, and their presence in scripture, are worth dwelling on, difficult as they are. These are the words of Holy Scripture, words many worshiping communities call "the Word of the Lord," words that have been affirmed by generation upon generation of Jews and Christians as representative of God's work in the world. And they are blaming God for loneliness. They don't describe loneliness; they throw loneliness at the foot of God and say, "God, why have you done this to me?" And this, we say, is an acceptable form of prayer. The Hebrew word for "psalms" is *tehillim*: praises. Somehow this psalm of desperation and loneliness praises God. We have permission, biblical permission, to cry out to God in the midst of loneliness and pain. God can handle, not only our feelings of loneliness, but also our sense that we have been victimized by loneliness, that loneliness should not be.

God does more than handle our feelings of loneliness, however. God expresses a radical solidarity with our experience and our hurt. In John 15, Jesus tells the gathered disciples:

> This is my commandment, that you love one another as I have loved you. No one has greater love than this, to lay down one's life for one's friends. You are my friends if you do what I command you. I do not call you servants any longer, because the servant does not know what the master is doing; but I have called you friends, because I have made known to you everything that I have heard from my Father. You did not choose me but I chose you. And I appointed you to go

and bear fruit, fruit that will last, so that the Father will give
you whatever you ask him in my name. I am giving you these
commands so that you may love one another. (v.12–17)

Jesus calls the disciples, the people he has gathered around
himself in community, his friends. We Christians make a rather
bizarre claim about Jesus, a homeless rabbi who was tortured
to death in a stinking backwater of the Roman Empire. We
make the absurd claim that in this Jesus we see the very face
of God. That is a shocking thing to say. It is so shocking that
the early church spent centuries arguing about what exactly
it meant. There was a lot of name-calling, a lot of excommu-
nicating and anathematizing, attached to disputes over such
questions as: How can Jesus be both human and divine? How is
Jesus, God the Son, related to God the Father? Did God die on
the Cross? We make the claim, the ridiculous claim, that Jesus,
the Human One, is also somehow divine, and that Jesus, this
Human and Divine One, called to himself a group of friends—
people with whom he intimately shared time and space, which
raises a question. If God needs friends, does God get lonely?

If, through Jesus Christ, God expresses radical solidarity
with the human condition, then surely God knows what it is to
be lonely. God knows what it feels like to need friends, knows
what it feels like to beat back the silence of seclusion and
gather companions to shed some sort of light into the darkness
of isolation. God hears and understands the broken cry of the
psalmist, "You have caused my companions to shun me." From
the Cross, Jesus cried aloud the words of another psalm, "My
God, my God, why have you forsaken me?"

"You did not choose me, but I chose you," Jesus said to his
disciples. Jesus asked the disciples to be his friends. Jesus was
not a distant figure on a pillar that others happened to gather
around. Jesus sought out friends. Friendship is a major theme
in John's Gospel. "The sayings on friendship in John 15 and
the vocabulary of friendship . . . throughout the Gospel,"

writes biblical scholar Sharon Ringe, "establish the relevance of the theme to the Fourth Gospel . . . [The] language of friendship sounds a persistent beat from the beginning to the end of the narrative."[1] She argues that the text is full of images and motifs of friendship "even when the language of friendship itself is absent."[2] For example, the Greek word *meno*, translated into English using a variety of English words such as "stay," "dwell," "remain," and "abide," is "like a red thread running through the Fourth Gospel from beginning to end," appearing at least forty times.[3] Jesus is interested in staying with, remaining with, being present with, the disciples—the divine presence in the midst of the community, a presence that stays and that will not leave them alone. If Jesus is a friend who stays, I can only imagine Jesus cares deeply about the lonely people of the world, like the person on the psych ward who couldn't name one friend. Not even one.

The experience of mental health struggles is often one of isolation and loneliness. Some of it is the internal experience of illness and pain, the subjective encounter with the symptoms of a particular disorder, but much of the isolation is externally created, imposed by stigma, misunderstanding, and fear. And as theologian John Swinton argues in his book *Resurrecting the Person: Friendship and the Care of People with Mental Health Problems*, the antidote to the latter is not medication, but friendship. "Running alongside the biological and psychological history of people with mental health problems is a form of social experience that is fundamentally degrading, exclusionary, and dehumanizing."[4] The church, therefore, has a vital role to play in the care of people with mental health problems:

> [E]ven in the midst of the most profound forms of mental health problems there is a vital relational dimension that is frequently *more* significant, from the perspective of the sufferers, than other factors within their illness. . . . It is here, within the area of personal relationships, that the Christian

community has a vital contribution to make to the care of people with mental health problems. The role of the Christian community lies not only in creating a context that will nurture relational development and enable people to find wholeness in the midst of their brokenness, but also in actively countering the wider interpersonal and social forces that act to stigmatize, alienate, oppress, and exclude many people with mental health problems from full social inclusion.[5]

Swinton articulates an important differentiation between Christ-like friendship and professional services aimed at people with mental health problems:

Unlike many agents with whom people with mental health problems may come into contact, the task of the Christlike friend is not to *do* anything for them, but rather to *be* someone for them—someone who understands and accepts them as persons; someone who is *with* and *for* them in the way that God is also *with* and *for* them; someone who reveals the nature of God and the transforming power of the Spirit of Christ in a form that is tangible, accessible, and deeply powerful.[6]

His words resonate deeply with me. When I reflect on my experience with mental illness, I am cognizant of many different types of support I have received (a fact that, as the opening story of this chapter helps reveal, cannot be assumed for many people with mental health struggles). I received professional support and services, and am grateful to have had (and to continue to have) access to hospitals, social workers, psychiatric nurses, counselors, and psychiatrists. I have also received the support of professional clergy, for which I—a lifelong churchgoer who was in seminary at the time of my hospitalization—am profoundly grateful. If anyone were seeking a guide to best practices for clergy seeing to care for those with mental illness, I would point them in the direction of those who visited, wrote, or called me while I was in the hospital.

In many ways, however, the most important support I received during my time in and out of the hospital did not come from professional caregivers, but from friends and companions on the journey. Some of them were seminary classmates or members of faith communities. Recently, I visited with a seminary friend who returned a stack of letters I had written to my seminary community from the hospital. Reading them almost six years later, I was struck by my deep longing for connection and relationship. I am grateful to have had a community to write to and reach out to. Others of these friends were family members, many of whom do not share the particular religious convictions that animate much of this book. A cousin wrote to me with words of encouragement and love, and pointed out how very intentionally religion was not a part of her life, though it seemed very intentionally to be a part of mine. My sister, not the most churchgoing of folks, sent me a letter with accompanying drawings that included this parable: "All forests need periodic fire to be healthy. Without fire to cleanse dead branches and leaves build up...and usually, because of lightning strike, there's a huge destructive fire. A badly burned forest takes awhile to recover. But it always does." The final panel of her hand-drawn comic was a small flower rising, beautifully, from a burned stump. I mention these letters because, while this book wraps itself in and out of themes related to Christian spirituality, my experience of healing and recovery also involves and includes people who would not call themselves Christian. I can only reject any understanding of healing, of wholeness, or of spirituality that would exclude these beloved companions.

Many of the companions who accompanied me on this journey were fellow sufferers, people who came into my life because of our shared experience of hospitalization and who, for the most part, have since departed my life. I am struck by the wisdom of those caring professionals who recognized our commonality and directed us, the oft-stigmatized denizens of the psych ward, to each other for learning and healing. The social workers at Sibley often reminded us that some of the best insights we would have would come from each other, which is why each day included group sessions. They asked us if anyone resonated with the words of the person who had just shared. At Silver Hill Hospital, group work in the model of the Twelve Step Program was integral to the program. Many of the patients there had what, in professional jargon, is termed a "dual diagnosis"—that is, both a diagnosed mental illness and a substance abuse issue. It's impossible to quantify how much I learned about life and healing from sharing in rooms full of newly sober addicts.

Of course, a certain level of care must be taken with the idea that the best healing comes from each other. Mental health struggles can often lead to poor boundaries, and self-care is important not only for sufferers but also for caregivers as well. Many people with mental health struggles are cared for by family members who could likely use much more in the way of professional support. All of these issues—keeping good boundaries, balancing self-care and care-of-others, maintaining one's own identity while seeing oneself intertwined with others—are the stuff of friendship. To speak of friendship in the midst of mental health struggles is to speak of a most vital kind of friendship.

Swinton proposes a detailed ministry model for "friendship-in-community" that includes community mental health chaplains, trained "friends," and partnerships between hospitals, congregations, and community organizations.[7] His book, along with many others, offers a useful guide to congregations asking themselves how they can best be in ministry with folks like me who grapple with mental illness. Having grown up in church, attended seminary, and spent much of my adult life asking questions about the practices of faith communities, I am glad to see such resources.

Yet, in my own writing and reflection, I am drawn less to questions about best practices for faith communities and more to questions about what faith communities can learn from the experience of the psych ward. If Christ really is present on the psych ward, then the Church, the Body of Christ, ought to be forming itself in the shape of that Christ. This shift, I suspect, would change how we think about church and about ministry. Just as it matters how we imagine God, it matters how we imagine church and ministry. It matters how we imagine who we are and what we are about in the world.

In an introduction to a collection of writings about images for the role of pastoral caregiver, Robert Dykstra writes about the "essential insecurity" of pastoral theologians: "It is hard to conceive of persons in other lines of work—construction workers, hair stylists, dentists, tennis pros, even systematic theologians or biblical scholars—bothering to concoct so steady a diet of metaphorical equivalents to their chosen fields."[8] He traces this fundamental insecurity back to the origins of the field of pastoral theology in the writing and thinking of a Presbyterian pastor named Anton Boisen, who himself experienced psychiatric hospitalization after a major breakdown.[9] But Dykstra ultimately concludes that the effusion of metaphorical responses to the question: "What is pastoral care?" are a gift, rather than a weakness—a true representation of the endless mystery and unending quest for identity characteristic of the human encounter with the divine. Such mystery remains resistant to technical fixes or three-step guides to success. Images of care and ministry

> function less as technical training guides or "how-to" manuals for basic counseling or crisis intervention skills than, as previously indicated, as works of art intent on inspiring ministry in more indirect and subtle ways. Like the evocative power of images in portraits, sculptures, films, or poetry, these pastoral images serve not so much to inform specific tasks of ministry, but to foster a richer sense of pastoral self-understanding, identity, and integrity.[10]

Dykstra writes with the trained caregiver—the pastor or the hospital chaplain—in mind. It is indicative of how deep the mindset of professional ministry is that an essay about the endless self-reflection and unstable identity of the pastoral profession would fail to notice its own deeply held presupposition about who does pastoral care—namely, the trained minister or chaplain. I say this, as a seminary-trained person who serves as a chaplain, with no sense of bitterness, nor any real intention to critique. This is simply Dykstra's audience. And I wonder what images of ministry might emerge were we to focus, not on the single professional caregiver, but on the community of mutual care and solidarity that forms, by necessity, in the midst of suffering. What does pastoral ministry look like when it is inspired by the Christ of the psych ward?

Allow me, then, to propose an image for ministry not *to* the denizens of the psychiatric hospital, but one that emerges *from* the psych ward. More accurately—since the idea does not at all originate with me—an image that powerfully matches my own experience with struggle, care, and healing during those difficult months, and that continues to inform my own approach to care and to ministry. To explore this image, we will return, again, to the Gospel of John and the same passage in which Jesus refers to the disciples as "friends."

The passage from John 15 I mentioned earlier is part of a longer segment of text (John 13–17) unique to the Fourth Gospel. While Matthew, Mark, and Luke all record a shared meal that has come to be called "the Last Supper," John's Gospel features an extended exchange between Jesus and his followers, often referred to as the "Farewell Discourse." Not solely an extended teaching, as in Matthew's Sermon on the Mount, the Farewell Discourse has a pastoral tone, addressing the deep concern of Jesus's disciples—his friends—about being left alone. The disciples fear not only sadness at the loss of a friend but also "the vulnerability resulting from the loss of a guiding force and advocate that is an aspect of their bereavement."[11]

Jesus assuages the disciples' fears with a promise. Though his departure, still misunderstood by the disciples, might be imminent, another would be sent by God to take Jesus's place. "I will ask the Father," says Jesus, "and he will give you another *parakletos*, to be with you forever" (John 14:15–16). I have rendered the word *parakletos* as a transliteration of its original Greek in order to emphasize the diversity of ways to translate the word. A rather literal translation of the word is "one called alongside." Around the time of John's Gospel, the term likely had secular and legal connotations, leading to the common translation of "advocate." "Comforter" is another common translation. One who is called alongside could also be a companion, one who accompanies.[12] So whoever or whatever this *parakletos* is, it is an Advocate, a Comforter, and a Companion.

So who or what is this *parakletos*? Jesus goes on:

> This is the Spirit of truth, whom the world cannot receive, because it neither sees him nor knows him. You know him, because he abides with you, and he will be in you. . . . I have said these things to you while I am still with you. But the Advocate, the Holy Spirit, whom the Father will send in my name, will teach you everything, and remind you of all that I have said to you. (John 14:17, 25–26)[13]

The *parakletos* is the Spirit. What's more, Jesus refers to the Spirit as "another *parakletos*"—the first one, we assume, was Jesus. The Spirit will advocate, comfort, and accompany Jesus's friends, just as Jesus did in his earthly life.

Jesus describes the comfort provided by this Spirit: "Peace I leave with you; my peace I give to you. I do not give to you as the world gives. Do not let your hearts be troubled, and do not let them be afraid" (John 14:27). Later, after Jesus's death, the disciples are huddled together in a locked room, afraid. Jesus appears to fulfill his promise, wishing them peace and breathing on them the Holy Spirit—the other *parakletos*—and sending them just as Jesus had been sent (John 20:19–23).

So we have Jesus, promising the disciples they will not be left alone, promising that God will send another like Jesus, another who will provide the disciples, his friends, with comfort, advocacy, and companionship. This Spirit of truth and peace is breathed on the disciples at the moment when they are sent out, in the same way that Jesus has been sent—as Word become flesh for the whole world. The image of the *parakletos*, then, the one who is called alongside, is both an image of the divine and, at the same time, an image for the church in ministry to the world. In John's Gospel, the community of believers becomes the community sent in ministry as a function of the gift of the *parakletos*, who is the animating force—literally, in John, the breath—of this new community. The Christian community can only be a living community to the extent that it is breathing in the breath of God. We are only a Christian community when the air that we breathe is the Spirit who advocates for those who feel silenced, accompanies those who are afraid, and comforts those who are afflicted.

I am not defining a list of things we "should" be doing as a community. It's not a legal code for us. It's not a series of programs. It's not even a normative guideline like the Sermon on the Mount or the ethical exhortations of Paul. It is our identity. It is who we are, who we are created to be by the Spirit, the breath, of the Resurrected Christ.

John's Gospel begins with a divine image, the Wisdom/ Word of God, that takes on flesh and lives among us as fully human. By the end of the story, the Wisdom/Word has taken on breath, and has breathed itself out among a new community to be shaped in its likeness as advocates, comforters, companions, and friends. These characteristics become a concrete, lived-out way of being in community with each other and, in particular, with those who are suffering, struggling, and, in one form or another, locked in a room and afraid to leave. Sometimes, this community of Jesus's friends is sent to provide comfort—concrete acts of care in the lives of people who

are hurting. That might mean bringing meals to those who are
struggling to care for themselves. It might mean connecting
someone to proper medical care. It might mean visiting people
in the hospital, or afterwards, in the period of lingering loneliness once they have returned home. It might mean caring for
families who are, in turn, caring for struggling family members.

At other times, advocacy is called for—speaking up and
speaking out on behalf of communities threatened with per-
secution or oppression. Sometimes, that will mean working to
change unjust systems that deny people access to the care they
need. Sometimes, it will mean sharing stories, being willing to
speak openly about mental illness and mental health struggles.
Other times, it will mean handing the microphone to those
who are struggling with mental health problems, allowing
them to find their own voice to ask for what they need.

And sometimes, simple accompaniment is what is needed,
a silent companionship that consists of sharing the journey
in all its struggles and joys. Sitting with. Listening, even when
there are no words. Walking alongside in a quite literal sense—
to that scary psychiatrist appointment, to the hospital again, to
the new house or the old house where the ghosts of loneliness
whisper from every corner. The community of the *parakletos* is
called alongside, called to be a simple presence. This, paradoxically, is often the most challenging act one can be asked to do.

For me, the image of the one called alongside, and the
community called alongside to be advocates, comforters, and
companions, is important because it emerges out of a community of care rather than from a professional standpoint. I do
not mean to criticize professionals, nor to exclude those with
professional skills from the community of care being imagined here. I want to emphasize that the Spirit, the breath of
Jesus, calls into being a community and sends that community
in ministry to the world prior to the establishment of the particular structures and definitions that later emerge from that
community. This distinction matters to me because many of

my psych ward companions, who were instrumental in my own process of healing (and, I hope, I in theirs), had zero interest in the ins and outs of biblical Greek. Some of them were downright skeptical of my religious inclinations. And yet, to accompany, to comfort, to advocate? My fellow sufferers understood these verbs at a deeply instinctual level, a level of survival. I can picture my group members at Silver Hill Hospital sharing stories of pain and perseverance forged in the fires of their addictions and mental health struggles, all of our faces marked by fatigue, despair, and the barest flickering of what might even have been hope. I can think of few better images to help me understand that first community of disciples, locked in a room, faces strained with acute fear and fatigue and—can you see it, there, just before Jesus arrives?—maybe, just maybe, the faint, nearly instinctual shimmering of hope. Named or unnamed, it is the look of a community being shaped by the breath, the spirit, of truth and peace, the Spirit who is called alongside and who calls others alongside to advocate, comfort, and accompany. Faith communities do, indeed, have much to offer to those suffering from mental illness. They also have much to learn from people who, out of necessity, out of even the flickering, faded flame of the need for survival, have been called alongside each other and are learning from each other how to be comforters, advocates, companions, and friends.

I think, often, of that activity led by the social workers at Sibley. I think of the downturned face of the person who said they could think of no supports, of no one who could accompany them in their pain. I think of the loneliness I felt on the psych ward, sometimes cutting like a knife, sometimes just a dull, numbing background to the experience. I think of all these things, and I pray. I pray for a Spirit who will advocate, comfort, and accompany. I pray that we will experience ourselves as called in that Spirit; called alongside the lonely, the suffering. I pray we will truly walk alongside those who feel lost, least, and last. I pray I will breathe this breath. I pray the

Church will breathe it as well. I pray that we can truly call one another friends.

Notes

1. Sharon H. Ringe, *Wisdom's Friends: Community and Christology in the Fourth Gospel* (Louisville, KY: Westminster John Knox, 1999), 64–65.

2. Ibid., 75.

3. Ibid., 76.

4. John Swinton, *Resurrecting the Person: Friendship and the Care of People with Mental Health Problems* (Nashville, TN: Abingdon, 2000), 10.

5. Ibid., 36–37.

6. Ibid., 143.

7. Ibid., 145.

8. Robert C. Dykstra, *Images of Pastoral Care: Classic Readings* (St. Louis, MO: Chalice Press, 2005), 3.

9. Ibid., 1.

10. Ibid., 12.

11. Ringe, *Wisdom's Friends*, 88.

12. Ibid., 85.

13. Both "abides" in verse 17 and "be with you" in verse 16 are translations of the Greek word *meno*.

7

Diagnoses and Demons

"Patient histories are stories," the latest psychiatrist said to me, as he asked me questions in a more free-form manner than the other doctors I'd met with. "I'm trying to write a story I like here. Stories lead, supposedly, to diagnoses. Diagnoses supposedly lead to treatment."

"That's a lot of supposedlys," I observed.

"Well, yeah. Because what? We have the Truth or something?" The capital 'T' was evident in his tone. I laughed, but wasn't quick enough on my toes to make the implied Pontius Pilate joke.

That was the first time I met the psychiatrist who diagnosed me with bipolar disorder, after months of guesses and shifting diagnoses. The conversation was not exactly an advertisement for the precise science of psychiatric medicine.

"What is bipolar anyway?" the doctor asked with a shrug. "There aren't just two poles. I believe in the Trinity. Well, worse than that. I'm a pagan. I believe in multiple poles." The theological jokes—the guy knew his audience—and the cheerful honesty of his responses to my questions were, actually, very helpful. For many people, talking to a doctor is intimidating. For me, a confused and struggling psychiatric patient, the intimidation factor was cranked up a notch. What would this new person say about the invisible thing supposedly going on inside of my body, my spirit, my mind? But here was a doctor, well-versed in his field, explaining to me that a psychiatric diagnosis involved quite a bit of storytelling. Stories lead, supposedly, to diagnoses. Diagnoses supposedly lead to treatment. And I know something, at least a little something, about stories.

What is the story that we tell about mental illness? Is it even an illness? Is it demon possession? Is it just personal anguish, best resolved with the power of positive thinking? The question of what story we tell about mental health struggles is an important one because, if it's not asked out in the open, we will never be quite clear what we are talking about when we talk about healing or recovery, either.

The idea that diagnosing mental illness was a type of story-telling was not what I had heard from other psychiatrists, and I suspect the reason is quite simple. The dominant understanding of mental illness most psychiatrists are working with is a medical model; for those steeped in a medical model, storytelling likely sounds a bit too ephemeral, too subjective, for the serious medical practitioner.

The medical model of mental illness is important. I am grateful for it simply because I have been, and continue to be, a recipient of the model's healing potential. I take medication to manage my mental illness. Currently, Lithium and Buspirone are my psychiatrist's drugs of choice to help keep my moods stable, and my mind, body, and emotions at some sort of peace with each other. Suggestions that drugs are for the weak or foolish, or that a good walk in the woods or run in the park is all the medicine I need to feel better, annoy me on good days, wound me on bad days, and, on mediocre days, are likely to lead me to climb onto one of several soap boxes I keep for just such occasions. The medical model also gave me language to talk about an experience that, as I have mentioned previously, often felt beyond my ability to articulate. To say I have bipolar disorder does not communicate everything about my experience, but it does communicate something, and that is important. It also helps me to make decisions on when and how I talk about my mental health struggles. If I had some other type of illness or disability—diabetes, say, or chronic migraines—I wouldn't necessarily announce it to strangers in a bar, or tell a potential employer in a first interview. Neither would I go to great lengths to hide it from friends or coworkers, or from my spouse. The language of illness gives me a shared context that is broader than my own experience of mental and emotional anguish to refer to when making decisions about self-disclosure.

The medical model of mental illness is important, too, because it is intended to be an antidote against stigma. For example, the National Alliance on Mental Illness (NAMI) website has this to say about mental health conditions: "They are medical conditions that cause changes in how we think and feel and in our mood. They are not the result of personal weakness, lack of character or poor upbringing."[1] NAMI not only insists that mental health conditions are medical conditions, but also contrasts this medical understanding with understandings that tend to shame or blame those suffering or their families. John Swinton, writing specifically in reference to neurobiological explanations for schizophrenia, explains how the "reasons for this major emphasis on biology are partly an attempt to normalize and destigmatize mental health problems and partly a response to the work of people . . . that essentially sought to blame the parents of people with schizophrenia for their condition."[2] In contrast to speculative theories that seek to place blame on family members or personal failings, the medical model offers an explanation for mental health struggles that focuses on finding cures rather than finding fault.

For faith communities in particular, the potential for this shift in understanding around mental illness seems obvious. When illness strikes a member of a congregation or their family, congregations know what to do, almost instinctively. Prayers are offered. Cards are written. Casseroles are baked and delivered. A pastor, or perhaps a trained lay caregiver, contacts the family to request a visit. And all of these actions are understood as an offering of care and healing for the sick person, not in contradiction to the advice and care of medical professionals, but alongside it. Often, if the family is struggling to pay for the cost of medical care, the congregation will take up a special offering to provide financial assistance. What most congregations *don't* do is inform sick people that if they just pray and have faith, they will be cured without needing to consult a medical professional. We don't tell people their diabetes is a result of personal sin. We don't tell people to just pray away their cancer, or that going to see a doctor is evidence of a lack of faith. Yet these are all things that people with mental health struggles often hear from congregations. Churches do not often deliver casseroles to the family of the child with schizophrenia.

Mental illness presents many unique challenges, not the least of which is the long-term nature of severe mental illness. Any critique of the way churches handle mental health struggles is bound to be a generalization, one that might ignore those faith communities who do, indeed, respond with care and concern. Not only did clergy and congregants from my church visit me in the hospital, but my pastor opened up her home to my family, allowing my mother to stay there when she drove up from North Carolina to be closer to the hospital. Congregations, in other words, know how to be communities of care for people who are sick. The medical model offers a healthier approach to mental illness, not only for the medical professionals, but for communities of faith as well. It, then, has much potential for good. It also has its flaws.

The medical model is, ultimately, a story—a narrative we tell about mental health and mental illness. Like any story or metaphor, it conceals even as it reveals, highlighting particular plot points or symbolic references while downplaying others. For one thing, the medical model has an individualistic focus on pathology, often failing to take into account both the contexts in which individuals function and the resilience and resources of individuals and communities. In order to diagnose a person with a mental illness, a doctor does not look into a microscope or send blood samples to a lab. A psychiatrist listens as a person tries to put into words an experience that is often beyond or below words. Then the psychiatrist attempts to cross reference that often fragmented story with a list of symptoms in the *Diagnostic and Statistical Manual of Mental Disorders* (DSM). This is the "story-writing" to which my doctor was referring, and it is not an exact science. More to the point, it focuses on a list of things that are "wrong" or "disordered" in an individual patient, reducing their story to symptoms and often failing to take their context into consideration. John Swinton analyzes some of the problems with this approach:

> The danger is that the interpretative power of the medical model comes to dominate all other understandings in such a way as to blind us to some of the highly significant realities that surround the lived experience of schizophrenia. . . . An overemphasis on the biological aspects of mental health problems tends to locate the persons' difficulties primarily within the boundaries of their own bodies. The persons' problems are *theirs*, and the treatment is focused on specific, neurobiological defects within individual people. However, bodies do not operate in a vacuum, and mental health problems are considerably more than technological problems that need simply to be solved through the development of greater neurological knowledge and improved pharmacological intervention.[3]

By focusing on individual pathology, in other words, the medical model ignores the relational context of the person who is suffering. It tends to treat the person as a problem, or set of problems, to be fixed, rather than as a whole person with resources and relationships and resilience in addition to their wounds.

The way we use the language of mental illness doesn't help matters. The language the medical model supplies can be a relief to the sufferer, but it can also be used to label, denigrate, or harm. We might refer to someone dismissively as "crazy," but referring to them as "a schizophrenic" is no less dismissive, even though it is medical terminology. At best, the medical model allows me to say, "It's not my fault I am feeling this way. I just have a condition." At worst, it leads me to say, "Well, I guess there's something wrong with me, after all." As a result, a model designed, in part, to combat stigma can actually, if misapplied, cause or exacerbate stigma. By focusing on pathology and locating the pathology primarily within an individual, psychiatric diagnoses can inadvertently increase the sense of isolation already being experienced by the person suffering. "It's not your fault, you just have a disease" is not necessarily received as the encouraging word that proponents of the medical model would like it to be. Since the reality of societal stigma continues to impact the individual—not to mention other societal systems such as race, sexual orientation, gender identity, or economic inequality—the person is left with the sense that all of their suffering comes from an invisible internal disorder when much of it can be attributed to concrete external factors. The medical model runs the risk of what pastoral theologian Cedric C. Johnson refers to as "psychoanalytic functionalism," that "divorces its study of the subject from the historical and political contexts in which they were formed."[4] In contrast, Johnson proposes an "integrative approach" that "entails assessing interpersonal dynamics, family systems, sociocultural systems outside the family, economic and political systems, as well as religious, spiritual, or other meaning-making systems."[5]

It's not that the biomedical model is "wrong," only that it can be reductionist. It can reduce complex human experiences into a mono-story that does not take into account the whole human person in their contexts and relationships. Reductionism can also go in the other direction, reducing the experience of mental health struggle to an emotional or spiritual problem and ignoring biology, which is exactly what the medical model pushes back against: "Mental illness is not a result of purely psychological or spiritual problems; it also involves the reality of a 'broken brain' that can be visually demonstrated by various brain-imaging techniques."[6] Reducing mental illness to a spiritual experience often results in telling people not to seek professional help, because, after all, they need only prayer and faith. That is harmful. Reducing mental illness to a medical experience results in telling people they need to seek professional help, and then offering no other forms of help—no care for their spiritual, emotional, and relational lives, and no exploration of the questions of meaning and purpose that arise from their mental and emotional turmoil. Swinton points out that many people who struggle with mental health challenges find themselves in a situation in which "the primary form of relationship that is open to [them] is with the 'specialist,' the professional who is *paid to relate to them*."[7] People suffering, particularly from severe mental illness, soon find their relationships sorted into two categories: those who want nothing to do with their experience of mental illness, and those who offer conversations that are clinical, utilitarian, and professionalized. Both are alienating and isolating, in the midst of an experience that is already alienating and isolating, which is the exact opposite of what the medical model purports to create, and it leads to frustrating, and often strange, conversations with the professionals who are supposed to be helpful to the person suffering. Take, for example, the routine psychiatrist appointment, which, on a good day, with my life bumping along without plunging up or down into the chaotic swirl of a bipolar episode, goes something like this:

Doctor: How are you doing?

Me: I'm fine.

Doctor: Are you having any symptoms?

Me: Not really. Life goes on.

Doctor: Are you taking your medication as prescribed?

Me: Yup.

Doctor: Do you notice any side effects?

Me: Just the usual.

Doctor: Do you need a new prescription?

Me: Yes.

Doctor: Great. Here it is. That'll be approximately $4,000, but I don't really know because I've outsourced my billing to a different company. Call them with any questions. Have a nice day.

I don't mean to denigrate the work of psychiatrists. Doctors are under an immense amount of pressure in the United States, and psychiatrists in particular tend to be overbooked and overstretched. There aren't enough mental health professionals to go around. You can see, however, that the above conversation does not provide much room for a complex or holistic understanding of mental health. And the outsourcing of billing isn't a fiction. I have dealt with it multiple times, always to the detriment of my mental health. One hospital repeatedly sent me notifications that I was past due on payments and that they would be sending the bill collectors after me. Each time, when I called to protest that I had, in fact, paid them, they explained they knew that, but that the billing company's records hadn't caught up with theirs. And this was a mental health facility, that appeared unconcerned with the mental strife caused by my receiving such a notification.

I've heard many stories of psychiatrists who dismiss or even denigrate the faith commitments of patients, sometimes even suggesting that religious practices are delusions or aspects of mental illness. I had one hospital psychiatrist take up half of a session criticizing the time I'd spent as a mission worker after college, using our time together to question my political and religious beliefs as I sat there, suffering acutely. Another psychiatrist, post-hospital, asked me whether my faith had kept me from committing suicide. When I said that I thought it had, he said, "Yes, I've often had religious clients who didn't commit suicide because they believed they would go to hell." That is not, at all, what I believe—in fact, that's a belief that I find harmful and toxic—but the psychiatrist didn't make much room for a deeper or more complex story about religious belief.

Of course, psychiatrists should not be expected to be pastors or theologians, any more than pastors should be expected to be psychiatrists. There are some wonderful examples of increasing collaboration between mental health professionals and people of faith,[8] although I sometimes fear that the collaboration is somewhat one-way, educating pastors about the medical model without a similar openness on the part of mental health professionals to learn the stories and perspectives of people of faith. But one need not engage in this type of collaboration in any formal sense to be open to the stories of people of faith or, more importantly, to be open to the stories of meaning, purpose, and identity that people, as whole persons, bring to the psychiatrist's office. To paraphrase Swinton, if we assume that mental illness is "nothing but" neurobiology, we miss out on the complex dynamics of the whole human being in our care, including their spiritual life.[9] If my psychiatrist was right—if patient histories, and the diagnoses which emerge from them, are stories—then caring for people means creating room for people to tell their full stories. And our stories include but cannot be reduced to our biology, our medical conditions, or our theology.

If the medical model is a form of story that conceals as well as reveals, the same can be said for any other attempt to explain the experience of mental illness or mental health struggle. The form of story that the church has at times told about mental illness has often been unhelpful at best and harmful at worst. "The rise of Christianity," writes Andrew Solomon, "was highly disadvantageous for depressives."[10] Solomon is one of many

authors who chronicle the role Christian theology has played
in stigmatizing mental health struggles. He argues that the
"history of depression in the West is closely tied to the history
of Western thought," from the ancient world through the Middle Ages, the Renaissance, the Enlightenment, and finally the
modern age.[11] He traces the stigma of mental illness back to
the Dark and Middle Ages, during which "depression was seen
as a manifestation of God's disfavor, an indication that the sufferer was excluded from the blissful knowledge of divine salvation."[12] "Melancholy was a particularly noxious complaint,"
Solomon observes, "since the melancholic's despair suggested
that he was not suffused with joy at the certain knowledge of
God's divine love and mercy."[13] The stigma remains, as does
the association with evil and even the demonic, as Sarah Griffith Lund points out in her book *Blessed Are the Crazy*:

> Many faith communities still believe and preach that men-
> tal illness is strictly a spiritual disease caused by personal sin
> and not related to biochemistry. . . . Some preachers insist
> mental illness is only curable through exorcism, explaining
> that mental illness is a spiritual disease caused by demon
> possession.[14]

The conflation of mental illness with the demonic is given biblical backing in many churches: "The idea that Jesus alone can
cure people of mental illness comes from an interpretation of
biblical accounts of Jesus healing people."[15] Writing about her
son David's experience with schizophrenia, theologian Rosemary Radford Ruether traces the resilience of the "theory of
demonic possession" as the source of mental illness, recount-
ing that at one point in his illness David actually decided he was
possessed and requested a meeting with a priest for exorcism.[16]

Let me pause here to say that if you have experience with
a church that told you your mental health struggles were a
result of bad demons or bad faith, or that they could simply
be prayed away, then you have been the victim of an injustice.

This is oppression and intentional stigmatizing—quite literally demonization—at its worst. I understand if this next bit is completely unhelpful for you, if you want to stay as far away from any talk of demons as you can. In fact, if you want to skip ahead, I will move on from demons after the end of this chapter.

I did not grow up in a church that associated mental illness with demonic possession. I grew up in a church that didn't talk about mental illness at all. The silence around the topic was, in hindsight, deafening. For me, the association of mental illness with demons was a liberating move, a way to bring the insights of my faith tradition to bear on an experience that, with no words to name it, was confusing and terrifying. "I am no Saint Anthony," I wrote in my journal, "and I don't think I will survive this." The note was accompanied by a stick-figure depiction of Saint Anthony the Great, tormented in the desert by a horde of demonic critters.

It wasn't that I believed I was literally possessed by evil supernatural beings, nor do I believe that the stories of Saint Anthony are stories about mental illness, anymore than I believe that every story of demonic possession in the Christian tradition is, in fact, a story about people with mental health problems who simply didn't have the scientific and medical knowledge we have now. Yet there was something about stories of demons and exorcisms that spoke to my experience in a way that the language of psychiatry could not. Whether or not it was the healthiest way to think, whether or not it was accurate, I can only tell you that, in the throes of my illness, I *felt* like I was being possessed. I felt like there was some outside force, or, if not outside, some not-me force, moving and pushing and prodding my actions and thoughts in order to do me harm.

In the hospital, I found myself reading the story of the man possessed by demons named Legion with new eyes. The story, found in the fifth chapter of Mark's Gospel, was familiar to me. As a young adult mission worker and then as a seminary student, I had learned to read the story through the socio-political lens of interpreters who pointed out that "Legion" was the name for a unit of the occupying Roman imperial army.[17] The story had political implications: a man freed from the occupying forces, the Legion, in an exorcism that included that death of hundreds of pigs—pigs that would have been tended to feed the decidedly un-kosher appetites of that same Gentile occupying army. The man, despite this possessing—this occupying—force, could not be kept chained, refused to remain docile, and resisted. His anger and pain were actually the sane reaction to the violence of occupation, revealing the subtle harm of his fellow townspeople's passive response to injustice. This is a powerful and valid interpretation, one that has particular meaning for people who continue to live under military occupation or the threat thereof. In the hospital, though, different pieces of the story stood out to me. The man is described as a burden on his friends and family, someone who wears people out with needing to keep him safe; "and no one," the story reads, "had the strength to subdue him." But they tried anyway, specifically because the man was harming himself: "Night and day among the tombs and on the mountains he was always howling and bruising himself with stones." Here is a man overpowered by an invisible but seemingly foreign force, harming himself, unable to be subdued or comforted, crying out for an end to the torment. After Jesus's miraculous (and surprisingly porcine) healing, the man is described as "clothed and in his right mind." When he begs to accompany Jesus, he is instead instructed to return home to his friends and family and share the story of his healing.

It is hard to put into words how very much I wanted to be clothed—in my own clothes, not in a hospital gown and missing shoelaces—and in my right mind, and to be sent home to tell stories about healing.

My story reveals how the same text can be used to create stigma and harm and to offer healing and freedom. People who are perceived by society as not being "clothed and in their right mind" can be outcasts, their condition simultaneously feared and normalized. The idea that their problems are caused by demonic possession, that they are in need of exorcism, can be incredibly harmful. And yet, the imagery and emotion of this story resonated with me in a way that clinical language did not. My internal experience of mental illness didn't feel medical; it felt existential. There is something powerful about the biblical language of demons and healing that is worth reexamining, even in an age skeptical of such matters. In his book *Reviving Old Scratch: Demons and the Devil for Doubters and the Disenchanted,* psychology professor Richard Beck reflects on his experiences leading a Bible study in a maximum security prison. There, he found, his own skeptical reaction to language about the Devil and the demonic bumped up against the reality of evil faced daily by the inmates:

I learned to get over my awkwardness in talking about the Devil out at the prison. Caring as I do about injustices such as mass incarceration, capital punishment, and all the other problems related to our criminal justice system, my concerns about social justice brought me to the prison. But once I was *inside* the prison I quickly discovered that my disenchanted worldview clashed with the spirituality of the inmates who spoke about the Devil and demons all the time. Behind prison bars, Old Scratch is real as can be. And I had to figure out a way to make sense of it all.[18]

Beck argues that, by eliminating talk of the Devil from our faith life, Christians in a post-modern context lose one of the core narratives of the Christian story: the struggle between Jesus and the powers of evil. This, in turn, leaves us without a robust spiritual language to confront evil and injustice. Similarly, I would argue, disenchanted and skeptical Christians often lack a robust language to confront the suffering caused by mental health struggles.

None of this is to say that we should return to a medieval understanding of mental illness as demon possession. At the same time, the powerfully evocative imagery of faith should not be so easily dismissed as delusional or superstitious when it can be a powerful resource for naming and healing. While Andrew Solomon does not hesitate to trace, in detail, the negative impact such theologizing of mental illness can have on those suffering, he nevertheless named his book *The Noonday Demon*, quite intentionally conjuring the connection between the demonic and the depressive made by monastic theologians like Cassian and Evagrius in the fifth century:

I have taken the phrase as the title of this book because it describes so exactly what one experiences in depression. The image serves to conjure the terrible feeling of invasion that attends the depressive's plight. There is something brazen about depression. Most demons—most forms of anguish—rely on the cover of night; to see them clearly is to defeat them. Depression stands in the full glare of the sun, unchallenged by recognition. You can know all the why and the wherefore and suffer just as much as if you were shrouded by ignorance. There is almost no other mental state of which the same can be said.[19]

Solomon's imagining of depression as the demon who continues to haunt and possess, even in the full light of a sunny noon, is a powerful articulation of the often-nameless suffering of mental illness. As he himself is quick to point out, the phrase is not his at all, but is rather derived from the Latin Vulgate translation of Psalm 91:

> His truth shall compass thee with a shield: thou shalt not be afraid of the terror of the night.
> Of the arrow that flieth in the day, of the business that walketh about in the dark: of invasion, or of the noonday demon.[20]

More modern translations render this last phrase, not as "the noonday demon," but rather as "the destruction that wastes at noonday," making clearer the parallel with the previous phrase, "the pestilence that stalks in darkness." As is often the case, the ancient text has insightful wisdom to offer a modern debate. For the ancients, there was no clear distinction between the plague and the powers that be.[21] It is the destructive capacity of the plague and the demonic, not the sourcing of it, that is of utmost importance. Notice, too, the reference in the Latin to "invasion," for the ancients saw, quite clearly, the parallel between the personal experience of sickness and possession and the sociopolitical experience of invasion and occupation.

It is perhaps no coincidence that this same psalm, Psalm 91, is one of the scriptures quoted by the devil in the desert temptation of Jesus. Early on in the first three gospel accounts of Jesus's life, Jesus is baptized by John. We are told that the skies open and that the voice of God declares Jesus to be beloved of God. Can you imagine that kind of assurance—a voice from heaven saying that you are loved, valued, cared for, and accepted? Yet in each of those accounts, Jesus immediately finds himself in a wilderness, hungry, alone, and haunted by a demon who is immune to daylight.

Jesus, we are told, was tempted by the devil. In Matthew and Luke, where we are given more details about his temptation, the devil quotes Psalm 91. Matthew 4:5–6 tells us: "The devil brought Jesus into the holy city and stood him at the highest point of the temple. He said to him, 'Since you are God's Son, throw yourself down; for it is written'"—and he quotes the psalm—"'*I will command my angels concerning you, and they will take you up in their hands so that you won't hit your foot on a stone.*'" Jesus's tempter says, in essence, "Have faith, Jesus. If you're so high, so beloved—if you're here, literally at such a high point, at the pinnacle of this holy place, go ahead and throw yourself down."

I don't think that the devil makes people kill themselves. I don't think mental illness is caused by literal demon possession. And yet it sure does sound familiar to me: a voice that can come to you even when you've just been told how loved you are, that can make you feel lonely and isolated, make you doubt your mission and your passion and your identity. It might not have horns and a tail and a pitchfork, but that voice is very real.

What is notable about the story, when it comes to how we relate to people wrestling with the noonday demon, is that the devil shows up to test Jesus's faith, and Jesus responds by saying, "Don't put God to the test." A test, as it turns out, is not what people need when they're feeling alone in the wilderness. They don't need a test of faith. They don't need to be told that if they just tried harder or prayed harder or thought more positively they would feel better. They don't need judgment. They need acceptance. Friendship. Companionship.

Testing and accusing are quite in keeping with the biblical imagination of the devil. The name Satan actually comes from the Hebrew, *ha-satan,* who was originally understood, not as the enemy of God, but as a member of the Heavenly Council responsible for prosecuting humans. The name means something like "the accuser." By the time of the New Testament, this accuser had come to take on an increasingly contentious, even evil, demeanor, but the implication was the same: Satan, or the Devil, accuses, tests, and opposes the person of faith. Contrast this image with the *parakletos,* the Advocate, whom I wrote about in the previous chapter. If the Accuser is the lawyer for the prosecution, the Advocate is the lawyer for the defense. To rely on the *parakletos* is to be reinforced against the accusations and testing of the demonic. To invoke Christ in opposition to the suffering of mental illness is not to ask for a magical exorcism, but to cry out for the accompanying and comforting presence of a friend:

> Unlike many agents with whom people with mental health problems may come into contact the task of the Christlike friend is not to *do* anything for them, but rather to *be* someone for them—someone who understands and accepts them as a person; someone who is *with* and *for* them in the way that God is also *with* and *for* them; someone who reveals the nature of God and the transforming power of the Spirit of Christ in a form that is tangible, accessible, and deeply powerful.[22]

The story I have begun sketching here—a story of the accusing demons of mental illness being cast out by the accompanying friendship of the Spirit of Christ—is not the only possible spiritual story to tell. Robert Albers, for example, writes of those suffering from mental illness as "modern-day lepers" with an "unsanctioned illness"—his term for "those illnesses in society that bear the stigma of social discrimination."[23] His metaphor calls to mind the healing ministry of Jesus, though, in the first century context of Jesus, the distinction between healing and exorcism is blurry. John Swinton, for his part, writes of persons struggling with mental health problems in terms of the poor, and the central place of the poor in liberation theology.[24] Monica Coleman critiques the combative metaphors we often use to talk about illnesses, and speaks of her own journey to "refuse to go to war against myself."[25] She quotes Parker Palmer, who in the midst of his own experience with depression was questioned by a therapist:

> You seem to look upon depression as the hand of an enemy trying to crush you. . . . Do you think you could see it instead as the hand of a friend, pressing you down to ground on which it is safe to stand?[26]

While Coleman can't quite bring herself to refer to her depression as friend, she nevertheless commits herself to "peaceful, healing language" and practices.[27]

I can't bring myself to call bipolar my friend, at least not at this point in my life. As you have seen, I use language of struggle and wrestling, though, like Coleman, I do try to avoid warfare language—language that, for example, Richard Beck employs in *Reviving Old Scratch*. But all of these different approaches take seriously the lived experiences, embodied stories, and chosen language of those who experience mental health challenges. The internal landscape of mental illness cannot be captured fully or expressed by clinical or medical language. "When I feel strong," Coleman writes, "I save the clinical diagnosis for clinicians who use it as shorthand to guide them in helping me be healthy. I don't think of myself as ill or disordered, as the dominant language in the field might indicate. I think of myself as 'Monica' who lives with a 'condition.'"[28] No matter what language we use, we are telling a story. Surely those having the experience ought to have a say in how that story is told.

What story do we tell about mental illness? A medical story frames recovery in terms of medicine, which can be a powerful, and useful, and good story. A problematic spiritual story can frame illness in terms of possession and recovery in terms of exorcism. More robust spiritual stories, in all their variations, can frame recovery in terms of presence, acceptance, and friendship. Perhaps, in the end, better stories are the most powerful healing, the most powerful exorcism, we have to offer.

Notes

1. "Learn More," National Alliance for Mental Illness, *https://www.nami.org/Learn-More.*

2. John Swinton, *Resurrecting the Person: Friendship and the Care of People with Mental Health Problems* (Nashville, TN: Abingdon, 2000), 78.

3. Ibid., 81–82.

4. Cedric C. Johnson, *Race, Religion, and Resilience in the Neoliberal Age* (New York: Palgrave Macmillan, 2016), 5.

5. Ibid., 6.

6. Robert H. Albers, et al., eds., *Ministry with Persons with Mental Illness and Their Families* (Minneapolis, MN: Fortress Press, 2012), 7. The editors are referring to a book by Nancy Andreasen, *The Broken Brain: The Biological Revolution in Psychiatry* (New York: Harper & Row, 1984).

7. Swinton, *Resurrecting the Person*, 83. Emphasis in original.

8. E.g. Albers et al., *Ministry with Persons with Mental Illness*, Mental Health and Faith Community Partnership of the American Psychiatric Association, *https://www.psychiatry.org/psychiatrists/cultural-competency/faith-community-partnership*; and the National Alliance on Mental Illness FaithNet, *https://www.nami.org/NAMIFaithnet.*

9. Swinton, *Resurrecting the Person*, 82.

10. Andrew Solomon, *The Noonday Demon: An Atlas of Depression* (New York: Touchstone, 2001), 292.

11. Ibid., 285.

12. Ibid.

13. Ibid.

14. Sarah Griffith Lund, *Blessed Are the Crazy: Breaking the Silence about Mental Illness, Family, and Church* (St. Louis, MO: Chalice Press, 2014), 84, 94.

15. Ibid., 94.

16. Rosemary Radford Ruether with David Ruether, *Many Forms of Madness: A Family's Struggle with Mental Illness and the Mental Health System* (Minneapolis, MN: Fortress, 2010), 70–71.

17. "A Roman *legio* was composed of about six thousand soldiers and an equal number of support-troops. To residents of the Roman Empire, the Roman legion symbolized the occupying forces whose power was overwhelming and whose presence meant the loss of control over every dimension of their own society. . . . Given the play on words present in the name 'legion,' one would need to ask if the Gospel writers are not also

engaging in political allegory when they speak about the people's fear." Sharon Ringe, *Luke* (Louisville, KY: Westminster John Knox, 1995), 120–21.

18. Richard Beck, *Reviving Old Scratch: Demons and the Devil for Doubters and the Disenchanted* (Minneapolis, MN: Fortress Press, 2016), xviii.

19. Ibid., 292.

20. Ibid., 293.

21. Walter Wink, *The Powers That Be: Theology for a New Millennium* (New York: Galilee/Doubleday, 1998).

22. Swinton, *Resurrecting the Person*, 143.

23. Albers, et al., *Ministry with Persons with Mental Illness*, 2.

24. Swinton, *Resurrecting the Person*, 13ff.

25. Monica A. Coleman, *Not Alone: Reflections on Faith and Depression* (Culver City, CA: Inner Prizes, 2012), 150.

26. Parker J. Palmer, *Let Your Life Speak: Listening for the Voice of Vocation* (San Francisco: John Wiley & Sons, 2000), 66.

27. Coleman, *Not Alone*, 149.

28. Ibid., 150.

8

No Pill Can Fill the Hole in My Heart

For six months, I watched the seasons turn from a succession of psychiatric hospitals. The week before my first hospitalization, a friend noticed that all was not right with me because I was wearing a long-sleeved hoodie in the anvil-like heat and humidity of a DC summer. I was trying to hide my arms, covered with cuts, burns, and bruises, and was filled with a simultaneous shame and a desperate hope that someone, anyone, would notice my wordless screaming for help. But, confronted by my friend, I denied anything was wrong. My mental illness was turning my body against itself. I ended up in the hospital, when a week before I had been with friends on a beach. I watched the summer storms thunder and flash from inside of Sibley Hospital, and I prayed for the rains to wash me away.

On the Fourth of July, my mom called me to wish me a happy Independence Day. I pointed out the irony of celebrating independence while I was locked in a psych ward. She thought about it for a second and said, "Well, happy co-dependence day then." I laughed out loud. Later, the nurses joked around with us about our good view of the fireworks; it's true, from the seventh floor we had quite a view of just about every firework display in the DC Metro Region. Someone laughingly suggested that we all go up on the roof to watch. Of course, you can't take an acute psychiatric ward full of folks with suicidal ideation up on a roof, even to watch the fireworks. The image was funny to me, nevertheless. I sent texts to friends who were downtown at the fireworks display, but they didn't text back; I wondered if

I had been forgotten, and then hated myself for being needy and clingy and wounded.

By mid-July I was out. It was a Sunday, and my mom went with me to an evening church service I had been attending that summer. I remember vividly the plastic bag I carried with my possessions from the hospital outtake meeting, and the feeling of the grassy church courtyard under my bare feet as I sat in the hot sun and laughed with friends. I was free. I started an outpatient program at Suburban Hospital, which had been recommended by the care team at Sibley. Outpatient was a struggle for me. The cognitive behavior therapy techniques seemed blunt, almost bruising. Friends gave me rides. I stayed with friends in Maryland for a time, took walks in the woods, and prayed and journaled in the shade by cool streams. I was healing. I was ready to start a new semester at seminary, start an internship.

By the end of August, I was back in Sibley. I remember the anger and confusion with which I entered again, this time for a week. A hurricane swept over the region and I watched it rage around the hospital, its violent swirling matching the motion of my heart. When I was discharged, a friend took me to a chapel service at the seminary. I hugged classmates, took communion, and smiled at the thought of being back to normal. But the anger stayed, as did the summer storms. By mid-September, they had followed me back into Sibley for a third time.

"This place," I wrote in my journal, "has become more home than home is." It was not a comforting thought. From the exercise room on the ward, where I often rode a stationary bike, forcing my body to move and to feel, I watched as a house was built across the street. At the beginning of July, it had barely been a hole in the ground. By the end of September, when I was released from Sibley for the third and, I hoped, final time, it was almost a completed structure. A whole home, built while I wondered whether I would ever really find home.

The weather changed. The mornings were often misty. The leaves were starting to turn. They would turn quicker when I headed north, but first I traveled south. My parents were taking me in until my next step could be finalized. We thought the next step was a recovery program at a farm in western North Carolina, but I was rejected from the program because of a too-recent history of self-harm. Then it was a matter of figuring out how to get me into Silver Hill Hospital in Connecticut. It wasn't easy. First, I applied and was accepted. Then my admittance date was moved. I panicked. My parents did their best, but I was too much of a mess for them to take care of—their adult child, rendered helpless by his own brain. There was a chance that, if we just showed up, Silver Hill's acute unit—their locked ward—would take me while I waited to get in to the longer-term residential program. We drove north and colder winds started blowing. Somewhere in Delaware I remember watching seagulls floating in the air currents over a parking lot. I thought of a poem by Howard Thurman: "As the sea gull lays in the wind current/So I lay myself into the spirit of God."[1]

We got to New Canaan, where Silver Hill was located, and managed to convince the intake nurses that I was enough of a threat to myself for them to take me in. "Jesus Christ," one of the nurses muttered when I removed my shirt for an exam. Fresh cuts, all over my arms, shoulders, and torso. What a mess. Autumn began and I watched the leaves begin to turn from the acute care unit. The locked ward had an outside deck that was caged off but with an opening to the sky. Though locked in, we were able to go outside for breaks. Everyone smoked. For the few months I was there, I took up the habit. To this day, the smell of fall and cigarettes takes me back to that deck, watching the leaves turn and longing for freedom. "It smells like autumn, and leaves, and cigarettes," I wrote, "And we all try to pretend that we're not in a cage. At least there's no roof, no roof, no roof. Who would ever think to pray for no roof over their head?"

The colors of a Connecticut autumn are beautiful, even from a psych ward. I woke one morning to see the early sunlight bathing the leaves in what looked like pure gold. But the leaves had begun to fall and the light begun to shift by the time I was released from the acute unit into the residential program, which meant a move to a big, old farmhouse on the hospital grounds where I would live with other patients and participate in an intensive therapy program. The seasons changed around the big old house where I learned about mindfulness and radical acceptance and emotional regulation and riding the wave. In the morning, the grounds were often shrouded in fog. The leaves began to fall into the stream that ran behind the house, and the image of them floating down the stream and into the pond and over the little dam became, for me, an image for my frantic thoughts. See the thought. Watch it fall into the stream. Watch it float away. It's not a bad thing, the thought. It's just floating away. Let it go. And the next one. And the next. November came. Then came snow. We threw snowballs at each other and shivered as we took smoke breaks. Winter followed us on our walks around the grounds. My last morning at Silver Hill was the second of December. I awoke early, before the sun rose. That morning I wrote in my journal:

> The dark trees are reflected in the pond—places where pre-dawn light is touching—and the only sounds are the water on the rocks, and the ticking clocks, and someone moving around upstairs. I have no idea whether I'm ready to leave or not, so I'm not going to think about it. But I know I will miss the physical beauty here, the sun on the water and the changing trees and the fog and the little dam at the other end of the pond.
>
> I take one last slow walk along the creek and around the pond to the concrete outcropping on the other side. Dead leaves and grass, covered with frost, crunch under my feet. The water in the creek, clear enough to see the stones and mud on the bottom, rushes and burbles over the rocks. Some of the trees, bare of leaves, still have red winter berries on

them—on the way back one is occupied by a lady cardinal cheep-cheep-cheeping, who flies away as I approach. I look at River House, see—one last time—the ivy climbing up its porch and the wall under the common room window.

Out on the dam, I watch the way the water flows, undulating over the rocks, rushing over the dam and foaming, almost yellow in color. Even this close I can watch the mist on the pond water, flowing over the surface and whispering of cold. My breath fogs to match.

Each walk I notice something different. This morning it's the massive pine—lower branches bowed or broken by our early November snowstorm—with the grove of spruces backed up to the house. It's the first time I've really seen them, looked at them.

It will be impossible not to miss the beauty of this place— the flowing water, the trees, the expansive grounds, have all had their own, slow healing effect. Just some time away from the city to rest and heal.

Today, I return to DC. Am I ready? The only answer is: turn your mind. Be willing to mindfully accept what comes your way. The important moment is now.

I did, indeed, return to DC that day. Although I wasn't sure of it at the time, that would be my last time in the psychiatric ward as a patient, at least up until the present day. I have no better idea what the future holds than I did on that cold December morning.

It was gray winter in DC. Upon my return, I learned I would not be allowed to begin a new semester at my seminary. One administrator told me that I would be a burden on other students, which—just as a quick tip—is a horrible thing to tell someone, even if it's true. I was devastated, but I didn't fall apart completely. I didn't have to be hospitalized.

Lent began, and I helped serve communion at the Ash Wednesday service with hands trembling, my body still not quite used to new medications. Winter slowly turned into spring. Summer approached again as a full year in my new life as one of "the mentally ill" began to come to a close. And life was still hard. I still struggled, every day. I still wasn't "recovered."

What is recovery? What is healing? Is there a cure for mental illness? Does medication work, and, if so, what's God got to do with it? If God's got something to do with it, then what is the medication doing? Is mental illness more like addiction, in which one is always "in recovery"? If so, what does "sobriety" mean? Six months in and out of psychiatric hospitals, and the years since, have left me with as many questions as answers, some of them seemingly so basic: what are we even talking about, here?

During my first hospitalization, I did not have a good sense of what healing and recovery might look like. In order to leave Sibley, I had to meet with a team and discuss my release plan. What was the transition out of the hospital and back into "normal life" going to look like for me? Release plan #1 involved medication and a psychiatrist to manage it, as well as an outpatient day program. The plan was simple: I would ease back into daily life, with more support, and I would start fall classes at the seminary, as I had planned to do all along. Recovery, then, meant "a return to normal life." But the only "returning" I ended up doing was returning to Sibley—twice. By the end of my third hospitalization, the release plan was much more involved, including examining options for longer term hospitalization and intensive therapy programs.

Even having these sorts of options is an enormous privilege in our current mental health care system. Some of my psych ward comrades left only to return to situations of homelessness. For many people experiencing mental illness in our country, incarceration takes the place of mental health care. The type of options to which I have had access and the family support I have been able to draw upon are products of privilege; the inaccessibility of mental health care for most people in this country is an injustice in need of correction. What slowly became clearer to me, as my family and I considered my options, was that healing and recovery would not actually look like a simple return to my life before hospitalization. This wasn't a hiccup. This required a change in how I understood myself. During my third hospitalization, I wrote in my journal:

> What's happening here is not just me needing to be safe. What's happening here is a complete shattering of my perception of myself, what I thought was my identity. I will no longer be a student, or a seminarian, or an intern, or a pastor-in-training. Instead I will be a patient. How should I think about this?

How should I think about this? I realize now I've been asking that question ever since. I still don't have a single answer. What I've come to, instead, is a collage of images, an improvisational jumbling of memories and texts and stories and ideas that, together, help me make some sense of this journey.

I am not alone in this struggle with identity. Drawing on the work of psychologists Peter Barham and Robert Hayward and sociologist David Karp, John Swinton illustrates the importance of the interpretive work being done by people who have been assigned the identity of "mental patient," particularly in regards to taking medication.

> [F]rom the perspective of the *person* with schizophrenia or any other long-term mental health problem, the meaning of medication is often very different. While one might assume that a person would be glad to take medication if it relieved the worst manifestations of the condition, this is not necessarily so. . . . The act of taking medication for mental health problems is a clear affirmation that the person has a stigmatized emotional disorder, and as such, requires a dramatic redefinition of his or her concept of 'self.'[2]

Research has shown that, while "the majority of people did not object to taking medication" as a way to mitigate their mental health struggles, people "*did* object to . . . the suggestion that medication was *all* there was to treating their mental health problems."[3] According to Barham and Hayward, "What participants looked for from psychiatrists was an approach in which . . . the prescription of . . . drugs was an adjunct to a psycho-social understanding of their predicaments rather than a substitute for such understanding."[4] For people of faith, we could add "spiritual" to "psycho-social" in the above quote. This is important because, in my experience, people of faith have an added barrier in their struggle to make meaning out of their newfound status as "patient" or "person in need of medication."

On occasion, I give talks to congregations or faith groups about mental illness. People generally want to stick around to talk, share stories, and ask questions. One recurring question had to do with medication. Different people ask it in different ways, but it boils down to, "I know that since I (or a loved one) have been diagnosed with a mental illness that taking prescribed medication is the healthy thing to do. I know it's harmful to think that if I (or my loved one) just prayed harder or had more faith that this would go away. So why does it still feel like prayer should make this better?" In other words, even for people who intellectually accept the idea that medication can be good and helpful, it's difficult to appropriate that fact at the level of meaning.

I understand where they're coming from. At a certain, important level, this is just a case of stigma doing its thing. Even if I don't hold the personal intellectual belief that positive thinking or prayer or "just having more faith" would make mental illness go away, there's enough of that kind of thinking floating around for me to internalize it on an emotional level. Folks who have decided that, even if we pray for a sickness to be healed, we should also see a doctor, find the idea that mental illness is somehow in a different category a bit stickier to overcome.

On another level, I think this feeling that prayer or faith ought to be able to get us out of mental health crises is worth paying some attention because mental illness really does go after us at a spiritual level, even if there is a biological or chemical or psychological explanation for it. When I talk about spirituality, a term that can be rather nebulous, I'm talking about meaning-making. I'm talking about questions such as, "Who am I?"; "What am I doing here?"; "What's my purpose?"; "What are my passions?"; "What are my deepest held beliefs?" It's exactly all of that—purpose, meaning, identity, worth—that mental illness attacks. While medication can defend against those attacks by restoring some equilibrium, helping us build our resilience, and moderating our out-of-control moods, it can't, by itself, do the hard work of healing the damage done to the who-am-I-and-what-am-I-here-for part of our lives. Medication *can* give us a bit of the stability we need to do some of that hard work. It is, as it happens, more difficult to engage in spiritual practices when your brain is trying to kill you.

I'm reminded of a passage from Barbara Brown Taylor's hauntingly beautiful *Learning to Walk in the Dark*. She speaks of sitting with her guides on a cave expedition in the sort of absolute darkness that can only exist deep below the earth's surface:

> When it is time to go, I follow Rockwell and Marrion back out of the cave again, thinking about what good guides they are. They kept me safe while letting me practice courage. They pointed me in the right direction without telling me what to see. Though they have been here many times before, they let me explore my own cave. Maybe that is the difference between pastoral counselors and spiritual directors. We go to counselors when we want help getting out of caves. We go to directors when we are ready to be led farther in.[5]

To pastoral counselors, we who grapple with mental illness or mental health crises could add therapists, psychiatrists, social workers—all the people who help us out of the cave when we feel like we're running out of oxygen. Ultimately, we need to do the work of going into our darkness, of poking around in it. Whether that's a matter of spiritual direction or some other practice of faith, it's only by going in and through that we can discover our true selves and begin to work out what it is that we are called to be. In the meantime, the medication, the counseling, and the treatment, help keep us from getting lost in the cave.

Since my first hospital stay, I have wondered how to make sense of medication through the lens of my faith. At the time, I pondered the concept of pills as parables of healing—the parable being a short story that, while pointing to the reality of God's presence in our midst, is not in and of itself that presence. At other times, I thought of my glass of water and handful of pills as a strange sort of sacrament, an outward and visible sign of the inward and invisible work of healing, somehow making present in limited materiality the unlimited activity of God. Monica Coleman recounts the story of a minister friend, who also suffered from depression, telling her to have faith, not only in God, but in the medication: "You have to believe it will help you. Or it won't. You're going to have to trust this, too. . . . It's not idolatry. If you really believe God is in everything, if you really believe that, then you have to know that God is in the medicine too."[6] As people of faith, it is good and right for us to wonder how to make sense of the identity shift implied in taking psychiatric medication. In 2011, I wrote a song called "Sufficient." One line I scribbled down in a journal kept coming back to me until it found its way into music: "Ain't no pill that'll fill this hole in your heart." That line is true. It takes a whole lot more than a lithium pill to start to feel human again. But take the pill, anyway.

Of course, there's more to healing and recovery than medication. Medication as a response to mental health struggles evokes a particular set of images and metaphors, as we saw in the medical model discussed in the previous chapter. In the medical model, healing often implies a cure, or, at least, restoration to a previous state of health. Broken bones mend; high-blood pressure is brought back under control by a mix of medication, dietary changes, and exercise; a person is declared "cancer free." The image is of a linear motion forward in time, disrupted by illness, but then restored to its previous equilibrium and direction. For those with mental illness, there are challenges in adopting this image. It's not clear whether there is any cure for mental illnesses, nor is it exactly clear when someone could be declared to have returned to his or her former state. Whether because of stigma, or gaps in our understanding of what causes mental illness, or because of the nature of mental health struggles, the category of mental illness seems to have a more permanent insinuation to it. What, for the person who has been told he or she has bipolar disorder, does it mean to return to normal?

My time at Silver Hill Hospital offered different images of recovery. The hospital certainly employs the medical model, with staff clinicians, neurologists, and psychiatrists meeting with patients, but it is also well known as a place of recovery for those struggling with addictions and substance abuse. Many of my fellow patients struggled with addictions and substance abuse in addition to mood disorders. As a result, the treatment programs at Silver Hill are intertwined with the twelve-step recovery model. Regular AA, NA, and other twelve-step meetings took place on the hospital campus. Many people are familiar with the aspect of twelve-step recovery that involves surrendering one's addiction to a Higher Power of one's own choosing. Perhaps somewhat less widely known is the day-by-day aspect of the model. "You don't have to stay sober for the rest of your life," my new friends would say, "only for today." One is not "cured" of alcoholism or addiction by the twelve steps; one lives one day at a time, with the help of a Higher Power and a supportive community of fellow addicts. One is never "recovered" in the past-tense. To be "in recovery" is a life-long journey, traveled one day at a time.

At Silver Hill, twelve-step spirituality intertwined with psychiatric medical approaches as well as with an approach to therapy known as Dialectical Behavior Therapy, or DBT. DBT teaches skills that can be learned and easily remembered by people in the midst of emotional chaos, and it provides a whole host of images to go along with these skills. We learned how to "ride the wave" of intense emotions, knowing that they would come crashing in, strong, and might even knock us off our feet, but that they would also subside and lose their strength over time. We learned to practice "teflon mind," not letting painful thoughts or emotions stick in our minds, but letting them pass like clouds in the sky, or like leaves on the creek that ran behind the transitional living house where we lived and learned. We imagined our "wise mind" as a stone dropped down through the murky waters of our thoughts.

Underlying the individual skills and images was an understanding of recovery as the ability to manage, rather than eliminate, difficult thoughts, feelings, and experiences. DBT teaches the practice of radical acceptance. There is no alternative world, absent of suffering. There is only this world. Once we accept the suffering of this world, we can learn to live lives in its midst. Related to this acceptance is the practice of mindfulness—of being truly aware of our feelings, our bodies, our thoughts, and the world around us in a given moment. Recovery, then, is not something experienced in the future, for as far as we know, there is no different future. There is only now.

DBT and twelve-step spirituality have different origins and different practices, but they complement each other well in large part because they share a common image of recovery. Rather than the medical model's linear motion—a disruption and a return to normal—recovery is understood as a day-by-day or even moment-by-moment acceptance of one's reality. One does not return to normal or get cured of alcoholism, bipolar disorder, or a personality disorder. One learns to accept a new normal: This is my life, the only one given to me. I must live it, day-by-day, moment-by-moment. And there is help available to let me do just that, and to flourish and thrive.

The idea of the new normal calls to mind yet another image of recovery, this one from the realm of biblical studies. My friend Mark is a chaplain who works with patients undergoing neurological rehabilitation. His hospital uses the term "return" rather than recovery, calling to mind the medical model, with its imagery of returning to normal. But in Mark's opinion, both terms are "rather unhelpful on the spiritual level."[7] He points to the theological difference between reorientation and new orientation, a reference to Walter Brueggemann's now-classic interpretation of the book of Psalms. According to Brueggemann, the Psalms can be categorized not only by their function but also by the seasons of life they represent. He names three such seasons: orientation, disorientation, and new orientation.[8] As Hebrew Bible scholar Denise Dombkowski Hopkins notices, however, "Brueggemann changed his original label from "reorientation" to "new orientation" for this season of life. . . . Why? Once you've been disoriented, you can't easily return to your former orientation."[9] Return might be impossible; but the possibility of a new beginning, a new season, a new form of life, offers itself as a gift of hope.

John Swinton offers yet another image of healing. Drawing on the work of Keith Tudor, Swinton proposes two continuums. The first, a "mental *illness*" continuum,

> represents the primary focus of the traditional biomedical narrative. The specific training, research, techniques, and forms of practice typical of mental health professionals result in a tendency to understand and define mental health according to the absence or presence of pathology.[10]

To assess this continuum, one might ask about the symptoms that a person is experiencing, or whether or not they are taking their prescribed medication. But another continuum, the mental health continuum, is of

> primary concern . . . to persons living with a mental health problem. . . . This level focuses on meaningful personal relationships, spiritual direction, the quest for meaning, a valued place within society, and so forth. Within this continuum, mental health can now be understood in terms of growth and personhood, rather than by the person's illness experience, which affects, but does not define, the person. It is then possible to define mental health in terms of the whole person, rather than simply one aspect of the person, or his or her experience. Mental health can thus be understood as a complex process of psychosocial and spiritual development, that may or may not involve the eradication of specific mental health problems. . . . Understood in this way, mental health is viewed in terms of a person being provided with adequate resources to enable him or her to grow as an unique individual and to live humanly as persons-in-relationship.[11]

These two continuums are obviously not entirely isolated from each other. Symptoms of a mental illness can be experienced as an attack on aspects of the mental health continuum such as meaning, value, and purpose, while a sense of failure or loss of direction on the mental health continuum might trigger the symptomology or pathology of mental illness. It's clear, as well, that there are not only these two continuums; rather, the image evokes other continuums, such as physical illness and physical health: "Mental health involves a complex and reciprocal relationship between the physical, psychological, social, and spiritual domains within an individual, so that the health and illness status of each domain affects and is affected by the status of the other domains."[12]

Swinton's image of two continuums is complex and dynamic. What I find most helpful about it, however, is the simple assertion that one can seek and find *health*—in the sense of direction, purpose, relationship, and belonging—even in the midst of an experience of suffering characterized as *illness*. One way this possibility embodied itself in my own experience was in art therapy. Throughout all of my hospitalizations, I found my encounters with art therapy to be some of my most personally meaningful experiences of healing. I'm sure there are many reasons for this. The tactile experience of drawing or coloring served as an embodied reminder of the goodness of touch in the middle of an experience that sometimes made my own body feel alien. The focus on process rather than result kept me in the present and gently undermined the perfectionist mindset that was part of what landed me in the hospital to begin with. Most of all, art therapy helped me discover that creativity, and the grappling with meaning that attends it, could still happen in and through my illness. I could create—I could *be* creative—even when I didn't *feel* creative. For me, that was like a revelation.

The revelation manifested itself in the "Spirituality Time" organized by the chaplain at Silver Hill. Rather than an overtly religious or spiritual discussion, "Spirituality Time" was something of an open mic. The chaplain introduced the time by saying that we all had spirituality and that it manifested in our capacity to be creative. At these weekly gatherings, I played songs I had written and received affirmation and support. But more than that, I saw my fellow patients and sufferers come alive. I heard people read poetry and stories, play piano and sing. No fan of Top 40 tunes, I nevertheless found myself crying when a teenage girl plagued by eating disorder and body dysmorphia belted out a pop tune in which she imagined herself, not as ugly, but as a beautifully bursting firework. The chaplain was right. By offering space for creativity, music, and art, she had facilitated a truly spiritual experience.

Swinton's image of a mental health continuum that stands alongside of and interacts with a mental illness continuum offers the possibility of exploring the depth dimension of human experience, even and perhaps because of mental illness. When I was first admitted to the psych ward, I viewed it as a practical disruption, a distraction from normal life. I thought I would get better and return to what I had been doing before, which included following my call by pursuing a seminary degree and ordination. As the weeks turned into months, and as I realized that even when I was finished with hospitals I would not so easily return to my previous path, the disruption became more than practical. It became spiritual. My suffering, I thought, was interfering with my ability to live into my vocation. And if I couldn't live out my call, why did God give it to me in the first place? If I couldn't pursue my purpose, what was the point of it all?

I found a different perspective in the last few verses of the tenth chapter of Mark's Gospel. Mark recounts the story of a man named Bartimaeus, who is physically blind but is, as it turns out, able to more truly perceive Jesus than the disciples. On the surface, it's your basic healing miracle: Bartimaeus asks Jesus to help him, Jesus heals him of blindness, Bartimaeus gets up and follows Jesus. But what struck me in particular, as I read the story on the psych ward, was the use of the word "call." The word is used three times in rapid succession to describe how Jesus interacts with Bartimaeus. Jesus calls Bartimaeus. Calls him to do what? Simply to be healed. Bartimaeus's healing seems miraculous and instantaneous— that is not how I experience healing. Yet the call to be healed is both a moment in the story and the beginning of a journey. At the end of the story, Bartimaeus gets up and follows Jesus, but, importantly, that is not the original call on his life. His call, at first, is simply to be healed.

The story traveled with me throughout my time on the various psych wards, and beyond. Called to be healed: here was a new understanding of vocation for me, one not based on what I could do or achieve, but based in a deeper call on my life, a call to wholeness. As I began to tell the story of my time on the psych ward, and to apprehend this storytelling itself as part of my calling, I was reminded again and again of this simple insight—an understanding I would not have if it were not for my experience of mental illness. My vocation is not primarily a matter of accomplishment. It is, rather, an opening downward to a deeper wholeness. I am—you are—we are called, simply, to health.

I share these different images not because there is one right, correct way to conceive of healing, recovery, or wholeness. There is, in the end, no single way to define healing. I find each of these different images helpful in different ways, and on different days. Some days I need the medical model to remind me to do the basic things to take care of myself—meds, yes; but also sleep and food and water and rest. The medical model allows me to understand myself as a "normal" person with a particular condition that needs particular treatment. It can be an encouraging image.

At other times, the DBT skills I learned and the day-by-day recovery model of the twelve steps are crucial for me. Each day, each moment, is what it is. I can accept that, and ask for the help I need, whether from a Higher Power or from a supportive community or from a body of skills and resources. I will always be in recovery, but there is no "always." There is only now. This, too, can be an encouraging image.

There are other days when I very much need the two-continuum model that Swinton outlines. I need to be reminded that there is a depth dimension to my experience, that there is meaning and purpose, vocation and calling, creativity and spirituality present and available in and among and through my struggle with mental illness; that I can still create, that I can still be called, even when I am quite sick. This, too, can be an encouraging image, indeed. In all of these images, and in many more, I discern an underlying voice. It is, I believe, the voice of Jesus. It is calling you, calling me, calling all of us, to come. Though we may not understand quite what it means, it is calling us to healing.

Notes

1. Howard Thurman, *Deep Is the Hunger: Meditations for Apostles of Sensitiveness* (Richmond, IN: Friends United Press, 2000), 202.

2. John Swinton, *Resurrecting the Person: Friendship and the Care of People with Mental Health Problems* (Nashville, TN: Abingdon Press, 2000), 72–73. Swinton is citing Peter Barham and Robert Hayward, *Relocating Madness: From the Mental Patient to the Person* (New York: NYU Press, 1995), as well as David Karp, *Speaking of Sadness: Depression, Disconnection, and the Meanings of Illness* (New York: Oxford University Press, 1996).

3. Ibid., 75.

4. Barham and Hayward, *Relocating Madness*, 61, cited in Swinton, *Resurrecting the Person*, 75.

5. Barbara Brown Taylor, *Learning to Walk in the Dark* (San Francisco: HarperOne, 2014), 129.

6. Monica A. Coleman, *Bipolar Faith: A Black Woman's Journey with Depression and Faith* (Minneapolis, MN: Fortress Press, 20160), 279–80.

7. Mark Masdin, personal conversation with author, May 13, 2017.

8. Walter Brueggemann, *The Message of the Psalms* (Minneapolis, MN: Augsburg, 1984), 19.

9. Denise Dombkowski Hopkins, *Journey through the Psalms*, revised and expanded edition (St. Louis, MO: Chalice, 2002), 29.

10. Swinton, *Resurrecting the Person*, 135.

11. Ibid.

12. Ibid.

CONCLUSION

Leaving the Labyrinth

As I write these words, it has been almost six years since I left Silver Hill Hospital in Connecticut—the last time, at least for now, that I've been on a psychiatric ward as a patient. Almost six years since I left that big, white house. I can hardly believe it.

I was thinking about that house recently. I was sitting in a room on the second floor of a farmhouse of a beautiful retreat center in the Shenandoah. The grounds were thick with fog. When you're in the mountains, it's not really fog; it's being in a cloud. A cloud on a mountain—a quiet sort of transfiguration. I looked out on the beautifully obscured grounds, all the edges softened, and remembered my last day at Silver Hill. How I walked around the house—the house where I learned about radical acceptance, and mindfulness, about interrupting the chain and riding the wave—walked around the house in the snow and the fog. I stared at the stream and the pond where I had watched leaves flow by, disappearing over the small waterfall, imagining them as my thoughts, free to drift away. I peered through the trees, now silently skeletal with winter, at the buildings where I had learned from newly sober drunks and meth heads and nervous teenagers with body dysmorphia and addictions to painkillers and middle-aged women with eating disorders—so many people old before their time, or worn ragged by time, honest in their presence and their speech. If we were a body, we were barely held together by the sinew of desperation, after the collapse of the exoskeletons we had grown in a world for which we were, somehow, made too fragile.

Today, I am not fixed. I am not cured. The sickness that was in my bones, my fragile skeleton that I held so carefully as I walked in the fog on that last day six years ago now, is with me still. I can see it out of the corner of my eyes, even on the good days. I can hear it in my voice when I tell people how good my life is. I am not lying. My life is good. It is very, very good. I am grateful for it. But my skeleton, even if stronger now, is made of the same bones. I sat in the farmhouse in the Shenandoah and, in between beautiful conversations with students I looked out into the fog, into the cloud, and I thought about Silver Hill. I thought about transfiguration. And I thought about a voice saying, "This is my Beloved Child." I felt a deep peace, there on the mountain. I'll tell you about what I heard, or didn't hear, in that stillness and silence some other day, some other time; today, I will tell you: Almost six years. And I still need such grace.

I am writing in the middle of a tumultuous time for this country and for the world. Some long for a return to a supposed past greatness. Others fear what this gaze toward the past implies, for the past was not so kind to their communities, their identities. These different views of history and different definitions of greatness are echoed in congregations throughout the nation. Some long for the glory days of the past, while others fear what this story of faded greatness implies. In a reactionary time obsessed with the supposed greatness of the past, it might seem odd to write an ode to vulnerability, weakness, and fragility. Allow me to state, as strongly and unequivocally as one can state a thesis about weakness and vulnerability, that the last thing the Church of Jesus Christ needs is a return to some mythic, triumphalist past. I have absolutely no interest in any narrative that wishes to make the Church or the nation "great again."

The Christ who I met on the psych ward makes the presence of God known in places of weakness, failure, confusion, and hurt. It is this vulnerability that saves us. It is this vulnerability, not an imagined greatness nor any form of supremacy, that the Church is called to model and to witness. The only God who can help us is a God with some scars. Such is the God we meet in Jesus who, appearing in the locked room to comfort those he has called friends, breathing upon them the Spirit who is Advocate, Companion, and Comforter, still bore the scars of his encounter with the worst of humanity. "He descended into hell," the ancient creed proclaims, conquering death by experiencing death. The God we meet in Jesus is a God with scars, and the Church of that God must be willing to show its scars as well.

In his book *In the Shadow of Our Steeples: Pastoral Presence for Families Coping with Mental Illness,* Stewart Govig quotes the Anglican priest and missional theologian Leslie Newbigin:

> The poor, the deprived, the handicapped are not primarily a problem to be solved by the rich, the comfortable and the strong. They are the bearers of a witness without which the strong are lost in their own illusions. They are the trustees of a blessing without which the church cannot bless the world. Their presence in the church is the indispensable correction of our inveterate tendency to identify the power of God with our power, the victory of God with our success. Because they keep us close to the reality of the cross, they can bring to us also, if we are willing to see, the light of a new day which dawns from beyond our horizons and which is close to us in the resurrection of the crucified.[1]

What Govig and Newbigin both point out is that the church is not simply in ministry to people who are struggling with mental illness, but it is also being ministered to by them. To be present, to be in ministry with people like me is also to witness to the ways in which God's presence is made visible and tangible through us and through our struggles, our scars. This perspective, as they both emphasize, runs counter to societal expectations about success and power.

None of this is meant to valorize people with mental health struggles. A person with a mental illness can be difficult to deal with. They can be hurtful in their speech or their actions. They can be devious, manipulative. I know all of these things are true, because they are true of me. There is a fine line, too, between mysticism and madness. I have met people who are haunted and terrified by religious delusions, and others who claim to have heard voices and seen visions calling them to a higher purpose. Perhaps my own religious ponderings are as much the former as the latter. I only know I have tried to communicate the truth of my internal wrestling. I hope I have written a book about discovering Christ on the psych ward, and have not, in any way, communicated that I think I am that Christ. Rather, the gospel of grace springs exactly from the reality that it is in the mess and weakness of our lives that God reveals God's self. The Cross is a symbol of horrific suffering and of human failure. The empty tomb, on the other hand, is entirely God's doing. We follow Christ to the Cross, to the places of pain and of failure, of despair and of human cruelty, hoping against hope, often hardly able to believe, that there might be a resurrection beyond it. This is the vocation of the church.

There are so many aspects of this vocation which deserve more substantial treatment than I have been able to give here, even within the boundaries of the topic of mental illness. As my experience was one of institutionalization, and of largely positive experiences with institutions, the very important role played by institutional abuse and deinstitutionalization in our nation's mental health crisis has not been fully explored, which also means that the experiences of homelessness, incarceration, and abuse that are the reality for so many people with mental health problems were not deeply examined. Missing, too, is a thorough analysis of our mental health system, and the ways that partisan politics and policy failures contribute to its systemic brokenness. For now, I can only say that the Christ of the psych ward is being crucified in those places of injustice and systemic violence. Yet, even without discussing the many concrete ways the church is called to respond to these realities, I can affirm the fundamental call of the body of Christ—the body that is there, broken and healing and resurrected, on the psych ward. This call, like the call of Bartimaeus, is to healing, wholeness, and health. The call is to reconciliation, the gathering up and unifying of the fragmented pieces of the world in the grace and the love of God. The call requires the vulnerability to approach, with a mixture of empathy and awe, places of hurt and brokenness in the world. This does not just mean congregations should start mental health ministries. Nor does it only mean that the church is called to follow Christ to the psych ward. Christ is already there, abiding with, bearing along, and sustaining those who suffer. No, the call on the Church is also to follow the Christ of the psych ward back out into a world that suffers still—to discover anew, again and again, the presence of Christ already there among the hurting ones.

I have already written of the rich variety of images of healing and recovery available for those struggling with mental illness, but there is one final image that, more than any other, I draw on to encapsulate and express my experience as someone with a mental illness. It's the image of the prayer labyrinth. A labyrinth is not a maze, but a winding path contained within a circle. The path leads to a center space. One prays the labyrinth by walking it: walking in with a particular question, or prayer, or seeking to release a particular set of concerns or burdens; pausing in the middle for quiet, meditation, and centering; and then slowly and gently returning to the world.

For me, the labyrinth has come to symbolize the journey of healing. It's not a linear path. There are times when it seems as if one is very close to the center, only to turn a corner and find oneself on the very outside edge. Then, without realizing it, when one feels so far away from the center, another corner is turned and one finds oneself suddenly in the center after all. I'm not certain, even as I share this image, what the center represents. Perhaps the image itself contains within it different understandings, different modalities of healing. I used to imagine the center representing healing and wholeness. Sometimes, during my time on psych wards, I felt as if wellness was just around the corner, and then, suddenly, it was as if I was further away from health than I'd ever been. At other times, when the wholeness I longed for seemed so far away, I would turn a gentle corner and there it would be: an opening, a space. I would journey back out along the labyrinth and find myself, once again, outside, in a place of struggle, illness, and hurt.

But the center is not always wholeness. Perhaps it is a holding space: a space of safety, of temporary stability, before a return to the risk and uncertainty of living in the world. Perhaps, the center is the psych ward: a place where I found, not healing itself, but rather a space to rest, to be safe, to gather the breath and the resources and the strength to return to the world. Yes. It's this last thing that feels true to me. The center of the labyrinth is like the psych ward. I experienced Christ there, in a way at least as powerful and profound as I have experienced in any church building. But one cannot stay in that center forever. One must leave the ward at some point. So it is good news that the Christ of the psych ward, just like that human born so long ago in Nazareth, is always up for a journey.

> I turn, and leave the labyrinth.
> I walk out of the psych ward.
> Christ walks with me.
> And is somehow already there, before me, in the world.

Notes

1. Stewart D. Govig, *In the Shadow of Our Steeples: Pastoral Presence for Families Coping with Mental Illness* (New York: Routledge, 2000), 101.

APPENDIX

Mental Health Resources

A discussion guide, helpful practices, and an updated list of mental health resources is available at *www.christonthepsychward.com.*

You can also use the website to contact me about speaking engagements or facilitating a workshop for your faith community, organization, or classroom.

There is a plethora of excellent resources for congregations seeking to be more inclusive of the voices of those with mental health struggles. A partial list is included below. Remember, the most important resource for those struggling with mental illness is people and communities who are willing to just show up, listen non-judgmentally, and reduce isolation.

Crisis

If you or someone you know is in a crisis, you can call the National Suicide Prevention Lifeline: 1-800-273-8255. You can find out more about the Lifeline at their website (*https://suicidepreventionlifeline.org*) and on the website of the American Foundation for Suicide Prevention (*https://afsp.org/*).

If someone is in an emergency and their life is in immediate danger, call 911.

Websites

Many denominations have begun developing mental health resources for use in congregations—check out the United Church of Christ Mental Health Network at *http://mhn-ucc.blogspot.com.*

The American Psychiatric Association has a quick reference resource for pastors and faith leaders: *https://www.psychiatry.org/newsroom/news -releases/apa-releases-new-resources-on-mental-health-for-faith-leaders.*

I highly recommend Mental Health First Aid training for anyone, but particularly for people like security guards, administrative assistants, church greeters, ushers, and others who often end up

being "first on the scene" during mental health crises: *https://www*
.mentalhealthfirstaid.org.

There are a number of organizations with peer-to-peer support
groups, such as NAMI (*https://www.nami.org*), Recovery International
(*https://www.recoveryinternational.org/*), and the Depression and Bipolar Support Alliance (*http://www.dbsalliance.org*). NAMI also has a
network specifically for faith communities called NAMI FaithNet:
https://www.nami.org/NAMIFaithnet. On many college campuses,
Active Minds organizes student support and advocacy groups:
http://www.activeminds.org.

Books

In addition to *Christ on the Psych Ward*, there are any number of powerful accounts from people with mental health struggles and their
family members. Titles that have been particularly helpful for me
include *An Unquiet Mind: A Memoir of Moods and Madness* by Kay Redfield Jamison; *The Noonday Demon: An Atlas of Depression* by Andrew
Solomon; *Blessed Are the Crazy: Breaking the Silence about Mental Illness,
Family & Church* by Sarah Griffith Lund; *Not Alone: Reflections on Faith
and Depression* and *Bipolar Faith: A Black Woman's Journey with Depression
and Faith*, both by Monica A. Coleman; and *Seeing Beyond Depression* by
Jean Vanier.

For congregations looking for practical models for ministry, I
highly recommend *Resurrecting the Person: Friendship and the Care of People with Mental Health Problems* by John Swinton. Sarah Griffith Lund's
Blessed Are the Crazy includes a step-by-step guide to starting a mental
health ministry in your church.

Ministry with Persons with Mental Illness and Their Families, edited by
Robert H. Albers, William H. Meller, and Steven D. Thurber, provides
pastoral caregivers with a practical guide to the diagnostic categories
used by modern day psychiatrists and psychotherapists.

A powerful liturgical resource for churches can be found in *Stations
of the Cross: Mental Illness* by Mary Button, available from Church Health
Resources: *https://store.churchhealth.org/products/stations-of-the-cross.*

For more resources, visit *www.christonthepsychward.com.*